ENRICHMENT ACTIVITY 1:
Keyboard Learning—Letters

To improve control of new keys and motions:

1. Key each line of a 4–line drill twice: first, slowly; then faster.

2. Key each line of a 4–line drill once more at a brisk but comfortable pace.

Lesson 2: e and h

e	1	d ed ed ded ded led led fed fed eel eel jell jells
h	2	j hj hj jhj jhj has has ash ash had had hall halls
e/h	3	e h eh eh he he she she shed shed held held shells
all letters learned	4	has a desk; he had jell; she has jade; he has half

Lesson 3: o and r

o	1	l ol ol lol lol old old foe foe oak oak solo solos
r	2	f rf rf frf frf jar jar her her ark ark jerk jerks
o/r	3	o r or or for for her her fork fork roll roll roar
all letters learned	4	ask for her; jar of shells; he asked her for a jar

Lesson 4: Review

home row	1	hj ha ah as ad ask has had lad fad jak all ask jak
3d row	2	ed ol rf of or off for fed led lead heed roll sold
all letters learned	3	ah ha; ask her; old jade; for sale; he rode a sled
	4	she sold a jade jar; he has old oak desks for sale

Lesson 5: i and t

i	1	k ik ik kik kik ski ski did did fir fir like likes
t	2	f tf tf ftf ftf the the toe toe dot dot jolt jolts
i/t	3	i t it it fit fit its its sits sits tilt tilt kite
all letters learned	4	he is too late; she took the ski; ask for the jade

Lesson 6: Left Shift and . (Period)

left shift	1	ask Jae or Hal; Jake had it; Kae asked to see Lars
. (period)	2	l . .l .l l.l l.l fl. fl. rt. rt. rd. rd. hr. hrs.
left shift / .	3	Jae has it. Hal said so. Jake left for Oak Lake.
all keystrokes learned	4	Lars had to take Hal or Jake to Jade Lake to fish.

To improve technique as you key the 5 lines, use:
Curved, upright fingers
Quick–snap keystrokes
Down–and–in spacing motions
Quick returns at line end–ings

Improve Keyboarding Technique

key words	1	is of or to ah so it do he aid she for the fir jak
key phrases	2	it is | to do | if he | or she | for the | all oak | jade fish
abbrev./ initials	3	Lt. Oates is to take K. L. to fish at Lake Harris.
easy sentences	4	Heidi did ask if he is to ride to the lake for it.
	5	He tied the skiff to the oak dock at the old lake.

1

To improve control of new keys and motions:

1. Key each line of a 4–line drill twice: first, slowly; then faster.

2. Key each line of a 4–line drill once more at a brisk but comfortable pace.

Technique hints:

- Keep fingers curved, upright
- Keep wrists low
- Keep hands quiet (al–most motionless)
- Use quick–snap key–strokes

Lesson 7: u and c

u	1	j u uj uj juj juj jut jut fur fur due due sue sues
c	2	d c cd cd dcd dcd cod cod cot cot tic tic ice dice
u/c	3	u c uj cd cud cud cut cut cue cue cud cud cur cure
all letters learned	4	Jack said that Ura cut her foot. I shall aid her.

Lesson 8: Review

e/h	1	ed hj eh he she the her due had has did sled shall
o/r	2	ol rf or for old fir oak jar oar rod ode roll lore
i/t	3	ik tf it fit sit kit tie hit tide site till ticket
left shift/.	4	I did it. Hal has the list. He is at Lake Lasso.
u/c	5	uj cd cud cut cur cue such luck ducks cures clucks
home row	6	as a fad; a lad had; asks a lass; had a jak salad;
3d row	7	ed ol rf ik tf uj he or it due sit dot jut kid lie
1st/3d row	8	Lucie just left to ski; Uris should see her there.
all keys learned	9	Hattie ties her skiff to the old dock at Lake Jud.
	10	Heidi just left for the coast; she is to see Karl.

Lesson 9: n and w

n	1	j n nj nj jnj jnj and and end end ant ant and land
w	2	s w ws ws sws sws wow wow wit wit cow cow sow sows
n/w	3	n w nj ws own own now now win win won won hen when
all letters learned	4	His dock can jut a hundred feet into the new lake.

Lesson 10: g and Right Shift

g	1	f g gf gf fgf fgf fog fog got got jog jog fig figs
right shift	2	ask Ella and Sol; call Ron or Sid; Cal saw a wolf;
g/right shift	3	Gig saw Rona in Ghent; Cora and Doug are in Elgin.
all keys learned	4	Jack signed for that file; Flo said it is now due.

Lesson 11: b and p

b	1	f b bf bf fbf fbf fib fib rob rob big big rub rubs
p	2	; p p; p; ;p; ;p; apt apt lap lap pep pep nap naps
b/p	3	b p bf p; pub pub dip dip bid bid sip sip fib fibs
all letters learned	4	Dejon has left us to work up at the big teen club.

ENRICHMENT ACTIVITY 2:
Keyboard Learning—Letters, continued

To improve control of new keys and motions:

1. Key each line of a drill twice: first, slowly; then faster.

2. Key each line of the drill once more at a brisk but comfortable pace.

3. Key each *sentence* as a 30–second (30") timed writing. Find *gwam* on each sentence.

30" *gwam* = total words × 2

Lesson 12: Review

home row	1	a hall; a glad lass; half a glass; had a jak salad
3d row	2	for a pet; he owes us; she took the; to go for it;
1st/3d row	3	Bo and Ric had punch and a big can of tuna at two.

key words	4	if he is to do it us or so go ah eh ha pa an of id
	5	to cut but and end own for pan the did big jak all
	6	sign work held with rush turn curl bunt pang their

key phrases	7	to do | if it | of us | ah so | or go | to do it | he is to go
	8	to cut it | an end to | a big jak | she did it | if she is
	9	to work | sign it | to flap | burn it | to land | such a cue

key sentences	10	Keith ran to the bus stop; the bus was late again.
	11	She rode her bike just to the top of a high ridge.
	12	Al led the first half of the race, then fell back.

| 1 | 2 | 3 | 4 | 5 | 6 | 7 | 8 | 9 | 10 |

Lesson 13: m and x

m	1	j m mj mj jmj jmj jam jam ham ham map map man mane
x	2	s x xs xs sxs sxs six six fix fix fox fox lax flax
m/x	3	m x mj xs am am ox ox jam jam six six ham ham flax
all letters learned	4	Bix just sold me a new oak chair for a high price.

Lesson 14: y and z

y	1	j y yj yj jyj jyj jay jay hay hay may may dye dyes
z	2	a z za za aza aza zap zap zoo zoo zag zag zip zips
y/z	3	y z yj za oz. oz. jay jay zip zip lay lay say says
all letters learned	4	Chuck sent me a pair of jade dogs by Zola Bixwell.

Lesson 15: q and , (Comma)

q	1	a q qa qa aqa aqa quo quo quit quit quay quay aqua
, (comma)	2	k , ,k ,k k,k k,k kit kit; It was Kit, Jay, or Al.
q/,	3	Ask Quin, Raquel, or Quig to take the unique quiz.
all letters learned	4	Zach took my new jet to see Quig, Flip, and Bronx.

Easy Sentences (all letters learned)

1 Jay is to key the quiz if he is paid for the work.

2 Cyd will go by the zoo to fix the ski for the man.

3 Mazie is to pay the six men for the work they did.

To improve control of new keys and motions:

1. Key each line of a drill twice: first, slowly; then faster.

2. Key each line of the drill once more at a brisk but comfortable pace.

3. Key each paragraph (¶) twice: once at an easy pace to master keystroking combinations; again at a faster pace to improve speed.

4. As time permits, take one or two 1' timed writings on each ¶. Find *gwam* on each writing.

Lesson 16: Review (all letters learned)

home row	1 hj gf lag has jak had jag ask half dash glad shall
	2 All glad lads had hash as a lass had half a salad.
3d row	3 rf ol ed p; ws uj qa yj tf ik peg got row fit dues
	4 Raquel has paid you the yearly dues that she owed.
1st row	5 bf .l cd mj xs ,k za nj am ax an adz man band cans
	6 Aza has a black sax. Dan can call all jazz bands.
all rows	7 I can make my next goal if I work at it with zeal.
	8 Keep hands quiet and make a low reach to each key.
easy sentences	9 It is up to you to set a goal and work to make it.
	10 She may make the goal if she works with good form.

| 1 | 2 | 3 | 4 | 5 | 6 | 7 | 8 | 9 | 10 |

Block Paragraph (all letters learned)

Do not quit as soon as you reach your first goal. Size up the next job. You can reach the goal for it, too; but you must do all the work it takes in the right way each day until you reach it.

Lesson 17: v and : (Colon)

v	1 f v vf vf fvf fvf via via five five have have dive
: (Colon)	2 ; : :: :; ;:; ;:; To: From: To wit: Dear Alice:
v/:	3 v ; vf ;:: Van and Marv have keyed In re: and Date:
all letters	4 Bev saw a quick lynx jump down from that zoo cage.

Lesson 18: Shift Lock and ? (Question Mark)

Lock	1 Ruth is both a CPA and a CPS. She has joined AMS.
? (Question)	2 ; ? ?; ?; ;?; ;?; Who is it? Is it you? Who, me?
Lock/?	3 Did you join AAA? Who won the rating, CBS or NBC?
all letters	4 Virgil Quin has packed twenty boxes of prize jams.

Lesson 19: Indented Paragraph (all letters used)

If I try for high speed, I must try to build good form, too. It just works out that the quick move is a part of good form. So next time I must go for the prize of speed with good form.

LEARN TO FIND GROSS WORDS A MINUTE (gwam)

Take a 20–second (20″) timed writing on each line. Your rate (gross words a minute, or *gwam*) is shown word for word above the lines.

NOTE: If you finish a line before time is called, start over. In this case, your *gwam* is the figure at the end of the completed line + the figure above the point where you stopped.

Answers
1. 12
2. 15
3. 15
4. 33

Progressive Line Length Sentences (12e, p. 24; 16e, p. 30)

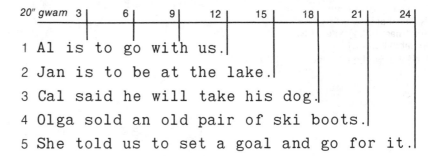

20″ gwam 3 | 6 | 9 | 12 | 15 | 18 | 21 | 24 |

1 Al is to go with us.

2 Jan is to be at the lake.

3 Cal said he will take his dog.

4 Olga sold an old pair of ski boots.

5 She told us to set a goal and go for it.

Self-Check Questions

1. During a 20″ timing on line 1 you complete the word *us*. Your *gwam* is _____.
2. During a 20″ timing on line 1 you finish the line and repeat it through the word *is*. Your *gwam* is _____.
3. During a 20″ timing on line 3 you finish the word *his*. Your *gwam* is _____.
4. During a 20″ timing on line 5 you finish the line and repeat it through the word *to*. Your *gwam* is _____.

Take a 1–minute (1′) writing on each line; find *gwam* on each.

To find *gwam*:

1. Add 10 for each line you completed to the scale figure below the point at which you stopped in a partial line.

2. The total is your *gwam*.

NOTE: If you take a 30′ writing instead of a 1′ writing, your 30″ *gwam* is your 1′ *gwam* × 2.

Answers
1. 9
2. 18
3. 18
4. 24

Sentences with Word Count Scale Beneath Them

1 Jorgie plans to find that mosque by six with Zack.

2 Maria Paso had a tea for Dr. and Mrs. Ruiz in Rio.

3 He is to work with us if he is right for the work.

| 1 | 2 | 3 | 4 | 5 | 6 | 7 | 8 | 9 | 10 |

1. During a 1′ writing on line 1 you complete the word *with*. Your *gwam* is _____.
2. During a 1′ writing on line 3 you complete the line once and repeat it through the word *for*. Your *gwam* is _____.
3. During a 30-second (30″) writing on line 2 you complete the word *Ruiz*. Your *gwam* is _____.
4. During a 30″ writing on line 3 you complete the line once and repeat it through the word *to*. Your *gwam* is _____.

1. Take a 1' writing on Paragraph (¶) 1; find your rate in *gwam*.

2. Take a 1' writing on ¶ 2; find your rate in *gwam*.

To find *gwam*:

1. Note the figure at the end of your last completed line.

2. Note from the scale under the ¶s the figure below where you stopped in a partial line.

3. Add the two figures; the resulting number is your 1' *gwam*.

NOTE: If you take a 30" timing, your 30" *gwam* is your 1' *gwam* × 2.

Answers
1. 15
2. 21
3. 19
4. 30

Paragraphs with Line-by-Line Word Count Column at the Right and Word Scale Beneath (16b, p. 29; 18b, p. 32)

Paragraph 1   *gwam* 1'

Do not stop at the end of the line before you make   10
a return. Keep up your pace at the end of a line,   20
and return quickly after you strike the final key.   30

Paragraph 2

Make the return with a quick motion, and begin the   10
next line with almost no pause. Keep your eyes on   20
your copy as you return to cut time between lines.   30

gwam 1' | 1 | 2 | 3 | 4 | 5 | 6 | 7 | 8 | 9 | 10 |

1. During a 1' writing on ¶ 1 you finish the word *your* in line 2. Your 1' *gwam* is _____.
2. During a 1' writing on ¶ 1 you finish the word *and* in Line 3. Your 1' *gwam* is _____.
3. During a 1' writing on ¶ 2 you finish the word *your* in line 2. Your 1' *gwam* is _____.
4. During a 30" writing on ¶ 2 you finish the word *no* in line 2. Your 30" *gwam* is _____.

---

1. Take a 1' writing on ¶ 1, then on ¶ 2; find *gwam* on each.

NOTE: Your 1' *gwam* is the nearest figure above where you stopped.

2. Take a 2' writing on ¶s 1 and 2 combined; find *gwam*.

Note: To find 2' *gwam*:

1. Note the figure at the end of your last completed line.

2. Note from the scale under the ¶s the figure below which you stopped in a partial line.

3. Add the two figures; the resulting number is your 2' *gwam*.

Answers
1. 15
2. 21
3. 17
4. 21

Paragraphs with Superior 1-Minute Count and a 2-Minute *gwam* Column and Scale (20d, p. 37)

                                                                    gwam 2'

          ·   2   ·   4   ·   6   ·   8   ·
Good form means to move with speed and quiet   5
    10   ·   12   ·   14   ·   16   ·   18   ·
control. My next step will be to size up the job   10
    20   ·   22   ·   24   ·   26   ·   28
and to do the work in the right way each day.   14

          ·   2   ·   4   ·   6   ·   8
    To reach my goal of top speed, I have to try   19
    10   ·   12   ·   14   ·   16   ·   18   ·
to build good form. I will try for the right key   24
    20   ·   22   ·   24   ·   26   ·   28
each time, but I must do so in the right way.   28

gwam 2' | 1 | 2 | 3 | 4 | 5 |

1. During a 1' writing on ¶ 1 you complete the word *be* in line 2. Your 1' *gwam* is _____.
2. During a 1' writing on ¶ 1 you complete the word *do* in line 3. Your 1' *gwam* is _____.
3. During a 2' writing on ¶s 1 and 2 combined you complete the word *of* in line 1 of ¶ 2. Your 2' *gwam* is _____.
4. During a 2' writing on ¶s 1 and 2 combined you complete the word *good* in line 2 of ¶ 2. Your 2' *gwam* is _____.

ENRICHMENT ACTIVITY 3:
Keyboard Mastery—Letter Concentration Sentences

Each sentence is "loaded" with the letter shown at its left. The sentences may be used as an intensive keyboard review by keying each sentence once. They may also be used for selective practice of the letters whose locations you are unsure.

1. As an intensive review of the alphabetic keyboard, key each line once. Repeat this activity daily until you can key the lines smoothly.

2. To use the lines for selective practice, choose for practice the line(s) emphasizing the letter(s) whose locations you are unsure. Practice each such line several times until you are confident of the key locations and can strike them without hesitation.

Lessons 20-25

a 1 Aida said her aunt gave her a pass to the theater.

b 2 Bobby bobbled the ball but went in for the basket.

c 3 Cecil can make a quick copy of the speech for you.

d 4 Dane held up a gold ring his dad had made for him.

e 5 Ed said to sit erect with the fingers well curved.

f 6 Flo left the file in the safe on the fourth floor.

g 7 Gigi said it is a good thing to go for a big goal.

h 8 Harl will help them with the new high school play.

i 9 Ivoni issued the invoice for the items you listed.

j 10 Jay jumped for a major jet job near the old jetty.

k 11 Kitty kept the cake knife in a kit in the kitchen.

l 12 Louis will key a letter and a small table for you.

m 13 Marv made a film to promote milk in major markets.

n 14 Nadia was near an open window when the rain began.

o 15 Odell holds the record for most games won at home.

p 16 Pedro placed the pad and pen on top of his report.

q 17 Quen has quite a unique quilt in his antique shop.

r 18 Rita had good reason to review the four new rules.

s 19 Sasha feels the system is sure to save some space.

t 20 Tod told the team that the outcome was up to them.

u 21 Urie is unable to give our full report until four.

v 22 Vivian said five of the seven voters have arrived.

w 23 Willa was one who saw how the two prowlers looked.

x 24 Xenia fixed the six tax forms to extend your time.

y 25 Yorba will stay on your yacht for a day if he may.

z 26 Zeno saw the zoo guard puzzle over that lazy zebu.

| 1 | 2 | 3 | 4 | 5 | 6 | 7 | 8 | 9 | 10 |

Each line contains every letter of the alphabet. Key each line 3 times: slowly; then faster; and, finally, at an in-between comfortable rate.

Alphabetic Sentences

1 Jay Witz asked me if Val Price got the quaint box.

2 Jane Glick did buy the quartz pin Wes Fox gave me.

3 Jeb Dietz could have Wes Kopf fix my antique ring.

| 1 | 2 | 3 | 4 | 5 | 6 | 7 | 8 | 9 | 10 |

50-space line

1. A 1' writing on ¶ 1; try to complete the ¶ before time is called.

NOTE: The ¶s are counted with superior dots and fig–ures to help you find *gwam* quickly; figures indicate 4–word intervals and the dots indicate 2–word intervals.

2. When you can key ¶ 1 within 1', proceed to ¶ 2 and key it in the same way; then ¶ 3, and so on.

3. Plot your best score on the 1' ¶ chart on LM p. 9.

For 2' writings:

1. Key the ¶s in pairs: ¶s 1–2, 3–4, 5–6.

2. Use the 2' *gwam* column at the right of the ¶s and the 2' *gwam* beneath the second ¶ of each pair to find 2' *gwam*: Figure at end of last complete line keyed + scale figure below last word keyed in partial line = 2' *gwam*.

¶ 1

gwam 2'

It is now up to me to push my skill to a new   4

level. I want a skill I can prize.   8

¶ 2

It is just not enough for me to keep pecking   12

away, day by day. I need to try harder, too.   17

gwam 2' | 1 | 2 | 3 | 4 | 5 |

¶ 3

I should try in the next few days to quicken   4

each of my motions. I should push them together,   9

also.   10

¶ 4

A pause to recall a reach, a delay in making   14

it, or a slow speed of motion will hamper me. So   19

pauses must go.   21

gwam 2' | 1 | 2 | 3 | 4 | 5 |

¶ 5

One way to shorten the pauses is to key from   4

copy I have keyed before. This offers me time to   9

think about motion speed.   12

¶ 6

Another way to force my speed is to key with   16

a pacer. The pacer does not stop, so I am forced   21

to race the clock to keep the pace.   25

gwam 2' | 1 | 2 | 3 | 4 | 5 |

KEYBOARDING SKILL
GROWTH CHARTS: 1-Minute Writings

Use in Lessons 16-75.

The charts given here may be used to record *gwam* on 1′ writings on straight–copy sentences and paragraphs.

To plot *gwam* on each writing to be recorded, place a dot on the vertical line at the point opposite the proper number *(gwam)*.

To show your skill growth, connect the dots with a solid line.

Some teachers and students prefer to plot a score only when it exceeds the last highest 1′ score.

1′ Straight-Copy Sentences

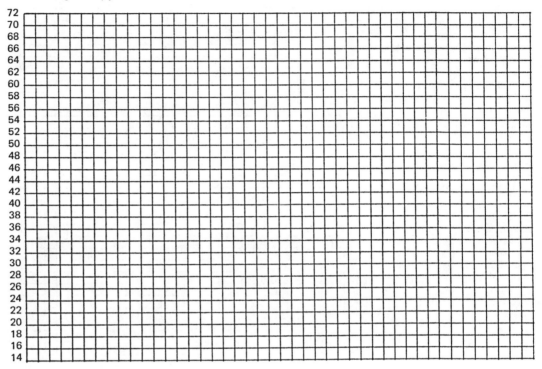

1′ Straight-Copy Paragraphs

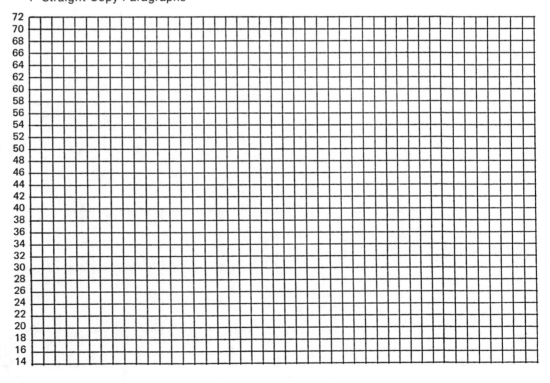

KEYBOARDING SKILL
GROWTH CHARTS: 2- and 3-Minute Writings

The charts given here may be used to record *gwam* on 2' and 3' writings on straight–copy paragraphs.

To plot *gwam* on each writing to be recorded, place a dot on the vertical line at the point opposite the proper number *(gwam)*.

To show your skill growth, connect the dots with a solid line.

Some teachers and students prefer to plot a score only when it exceeds the last highest 2' or 3' score.

2' Straight-Copy Paragraph Writings

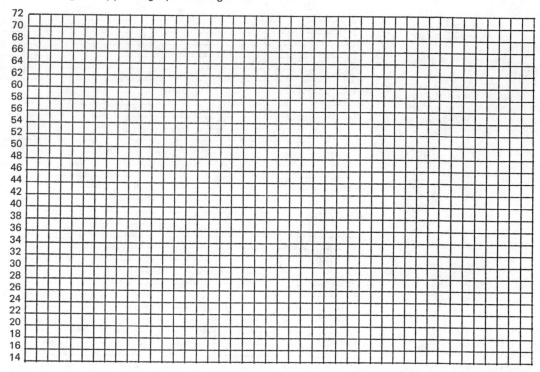

3' Straight-Copy Paragraph Writings

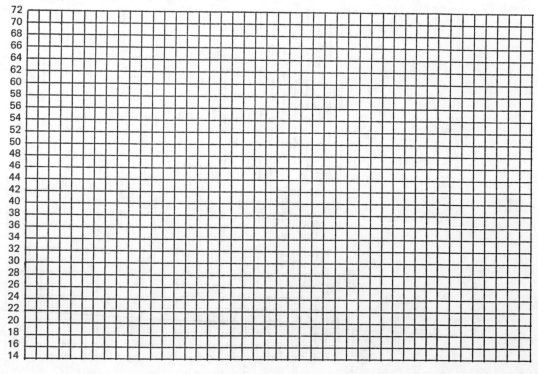

50-space line
each line twice SS
(slowly, then faster);
DS between 4-line
groups

Technique goals
Lines 1-2: Finger
action; no hand
movement.
Lines 3-4: Quick-snap
strokes; no forward
motion of hands.
Lines 5-6: Curl finger
down to bottom row;
quiet hands.

Technique goals
- quick, down-and-in
  motion of spacing
  thumb
- thumb held low over
  space bar when not
  spacing
- minimum hand
  motion

Keyboarding/Reach Review

home row
1 hj jhj gf fgf jag hag lag gas flag glad slag glass
2 Ladd has had a sad fall. A lass has a glass flag.

home/3d
3 qa p; ws ol ed ik rf uj tf yj fir due row pay quit
4 Luis took the white horse; Jae rode the dark gray.

home/1st
5 za .l xs ,k cd mj vf nj bf ox can van man bad jazz
6 Max said a jazz band cancelled and gave back cash.

Space Bar

short words
1 if so an is or am to me pa do it ma ox by we up as
2 he the and for off cut man but may bid fog row pen

phrases
3 to us|to me|if he|an ox|of it|to my|at six|was odd
4 he may|to pay|buy it|she is|of the|at six|it is my

sentences
5 She is to go to the city by bus to sign the forms.
6 Sheri may go with us to the town down by the lake.

| 1 | 2 | 3 | 4 | 5 | 6 | 7 | 8 | 9 | 10 |

Technique goals
- strike center of shift
  keys with tips of little
  fingers
- reach to shift keys
  without moving
  hands or elbows
- shift-key-release
  without pausing be-
  fore or after the
  shift-key stroke

Shift Keys

left
1 Jan and Hal; Nan or Ian; Pam is to see Jay at six.
2 Nate told Jane he saw the doe at dawn at Oak Lake.

right
3 Flo and Sid; Rod or Sol; Toby has left for Boston.
4 Roy will work for Rona while she is in Fort Worth.

both
5 Nana and Will left for the show with Flo and Jeff.
6 Cory and Risa will star in the show at Hakes Hall.

Technique goals
- return without paus-
  ing at the end of the
  line
- begin new line as
  soon as element (or
  cursor) reaches left
  margin stop
- make quick return
  movements without
  waste motions

Return

1 He is to go
2 to the inn.

3 She will ride
4 the new jets.

5 Donna said that
6 she is to work.

7 Joe still has the
8 flag that he won.

9 Laura saw that show
10 at the new theater.

ENRICHMENT ACTIVITY 5:
Technique Improvement, continued

50-space line
Rows and Fingers
1. Key each line twice: first, slowly; then faster.
2. Key each line once more at a brisk but steady pace.

Rows

home/3d 1 low jet apt fur yes dog kit has wig gold half quit
home/1st 2 man lax van lab ham can hag ban zag jazz call lack
all rows 3 zoo hex cud vim fizz quip joke busy next land grow

Fingers

1st/2d 1 as ax oz. saw pop lax sop low zap was lop zip aqua
3d/4th 2 if me it by us jut fit rub fur did vie yet but kit
all fingers 3 but men six for they quiz paid with dive jack flag

Response Patterns
1. Key lines 1–4 of each drill twice: first, slowly; then faster.
2. Take a 1' writing on line 5, then on line 6, of each drill. Find *gwam* on each line.
3. Compare better *gwam* on each drill; then practice lines 5 and 6 of the 2 drills that were slower.

Letter Response (think-say-key letter by letter)

words 1 as in we my at you few him are join debt only date
      2 ax on ad no be hum sat pin red milk care limp vase

phrases 3 a red mill | get my axe | are in debt | set up a gas tax
        4 be at my gate | sat on a crate | you see him in my car

sentences 5 A limp red lily was in a pink vase on a card case.
          6 As you join him, only a few states are in my debt.

| 1 | 2 | 3 | 4 | 5 | 6 | 7 | 8 | 9 | 10 |

Word Response (think-say-key word by word)

words 1 if to is so for and she did the six lend form girl
      2 an and for the she but may pan wit lay men sob jam

phrases 3 to do it|is to go|if it is|it is so|he is to do it
        4 it is she|he may go|all of us|she may do|is for us

sentences 5 She did lend all the audit forms to the six girls.
          6 Eight of the men may go to the city for the audit.

| 1 | 2 | 3 | 4 | 5 | 6 | 7 | 8 | 9 | 10 |

Combination Response (alternate word/letter responses)

words 1 if be is we of in may was the joy they data theirs
      2 as due pin for was dug him fit pop man art bid gas

phrases 3 so as|if we|is on|to be|go in|due him|the oil work
        4 to him|for gas|dug up|the art|she was|the due date

sentences 5 If you dig up the right data, we may end the case.
          6 You may be sorry if we all join in their ceremony.

| 1 | 2 | 3 | 4 | 5 | 6 | 7 | 8 | 9 | 10 |

TECHNIQUE CHECK SHEET

Excellent . . . . 4 points
Good . . . . . . 3 points
Average . . . . 2 points
Acceptable . . . 1 point

	Rating periods											
	1	2	3	4	5	6	7	8	9	10	11	12

Position at machine . . . . | Rating

1. Sits in a comfortable, relaxed position
   directly in front of machine. . . . .
2. Keeps feet on floor for proper body balance. . . . .
3. Keeps elbows in relaxed, natural position at sides
   of body to provide correct hand position. . . . .
4. Keeps wrists low and relaxed, but off frame of machine . . .
5. Keeps fingers curved, upright, and in keyboarding position. . . .

Keystroking . . . . | Rating

1. Keeps fingers curved and upright over home keys. . . . . . .
2. Makes quick, snappy keystrokes with immediate key release. . .
3. Maintains uniform keystroking action (force). . . . .
4. Keeps hands and arms quiet, wrists low. . . . .
5. Strikes each key with proper finger. . . . .

Space bar . . . . | Rating

1. Keeps right thumb curved—on or close to space bar. . . . . . .
2. Strikes space bar with a quick, down-and-in (toward palm)
   motion of right thumb. . . . .
3. Releases space bar instantly. . . . .
4. Does not pause before or after spacing stroke. . . . .

Element (cursor) return . . . . | Rating

1. Returns quickly at ends of lines. . . . .
   Manual: Quick, flick-of-hand motion. . . . .
   Electric/Electronic: Quick, little finger reach. . . . .
2. Keeps eyes on copy during and following return. . . . .
3. Starts new line without break or pause. . . . .

Shift keys . . . . | Rating

1. Reaches quickly with little fingers;
   keeps other fingers in keyboarding (home-key) position. . .
2. Holds shift key all the way down as the letter key
   is struck—capitals are uniformly on the line of writing. . . .
3. Releases shift key quickly after letter is struck. . . . .
4. Does not pause before or after shift-key stroke. . . . .

Tabulator key or bar . . . . | Rating

1. Reaches quickly with controlling finger; keeps other fingers
   near keying (home-key) position. . . . .
2. Uses minimum hand and arm motion. . . . .
3. Continues keying immediately after tabulating—
   without pause or interruption. . . . .

RATINGS

Excellent . . . . 4 points
Good . . . . . 3 points
Average . . . . 2 points
Acceptable . . . 1 point

Rating periods											
1	2	3	4	5	6	7	8	9	10	11	12

Reading/keyboarding response patterns. . .   Rating

1. Keeps eyes on copy—concentrates. . . . .
2. Keeps element (cursor) moving without jerks and
   pauses—maintains continuous keystroking
   by reading slightly ahead in the copy. . . . .
3. Keys one-hand letter combinations and words quickly
   and with keystroking action in fingers. . . . .
4. Keys balanced-hand words by *word* response. . . . .
5. Uses a smooth, fluent rhythm pattern which varies
   according to difficulty of copy being keyed. . . . .

Mind-set.   Rating

1. Follows directions carefully. . . . .
2. Gives attention to technique cues and goals. . . . .
3. Makes effort to reach suggested goals. . . . .
4. Practices with a purpose at assigned practice level. . . . . .
5. Shows alert attention, but shows no evidence of tenseness
   in shoulders, arms, and hands. . . . .

SUGGESTED EVALUATION/GRADING PLAN

1. Observe and rate the student on each major technique
   listed on this Check Sheet (or those that are currently
   appropriate), using point scores of 4 = A; 3 = B; 2 = C;
   1 = D. Enter the appropriate point score opposite the word
   Rating for each technique being rated.

2. When observing and rating the student, place a check
   mark opposite each numbered item that needs immediate
   improvement.

3. After all currently appropriate techniques have been
   evaluated and rated, enter the *Rating* scores in a table
   such as the one illustrated below.

Grade range
A = 3.6–4.0
B = 2.6–3.5
C = 1.6–2.5
D = 0.6–1.5
F = 0–0.5

4. Add (across) the *Rating* scores awarded the student for
   each technique and enter the total in the *Total* column
   opposite the student's name.

5. Divide the total by the number of techniques rated (8 in the
   illustrative examples) and enter the average in the *Average*
   column opposite the student's name.

6. Award A-B-C-D-F grades on the basis of the *Grading range*
   scale given in the block above.

Name of student	Position	Essential Motions					Response patterns	Mind-set	Total	Average
		Key-stroking	Space bar	Return	Shift keys	Tabu-lator				
Anglin, Sue	4	4	2	3	4	4	3	4	28	3.5
Bucerias, Juan	3	3	3	4	3	3	2	3	24	3.0
Cantrell, Tina	2	2	1	1	2	1	1	2	12	1.5
Donetti, Mike	2	3	2	2	3	3	3	3	21	2.6

Letter-Concentration Drill
50-space line; SS

1. For intensive keyboard review, key each line of the drill once.

2. For selective practice, select from the drill the lines loaded with the letters with which you are still having difficulty. Key each line twice: first, slowly to reestablish the reach; again at a faster pace to improve speed.

Letter-Concentration Drill

a 1 Alan may have to take a boat to the small islands.
b 2 Bobbi brought big boxes of books for a hobby sale.
c 3 Cincy can cash this check at a branch in the city.
d 4 David tied up that dinghy and moved down the dock.
e 5 Ed makes very few errors even when he keys tables.
f 6 Flora often fishes for catfish off the first pier.
g 7 Gigi has gone to get gift wrap for a huge package.
h 8 Hugh has to help his father fix the eight shelves.

i 9 Ivan is in the city to paint big signs for the firm.
j 10 Julie just took major prizes for jams and jellies.
k 11 Kitty knows the knife to use to cut the kiwi cake.
l 12 Lendl may sell the old logging mill near the levy.
m 13 Mel may make the men come to the camp for payment.
n 14 Nan can handle the land auction near the new town.
o 15 Opal took an option to buy the condo on the ocean.
p 16 Paula put special door prizes on top of the piano.

q 17 Quade was quick to quiz a quiet man at the mosque.
r 18 Rod rode the surf as it broke in toward the shore.
s 19 Susi said she was sad to see the summer slip away.
t 20 Todd got the teak table at a little store in town.
u 21 Ursula, your aunt urged us to rush the urn to you.
v 22 Vi has a very heavy velvet vest in her moving van.
w 23 Wes works with the two new women in the west wing.
x 24 Xavier is next of six to try to fix the bent axle.

y 25 Yuris says he has a yen for young turkey and yams.
z 26 Zumi was puzzled by the bizarre man in the bazaar.

| 1 | 2 | 3 | 4 | 5 | 6 | 7 | 8 | 9 | 10 |

Alphabetic Paragraphs
50-space line; DS

1. Key each ¶ once at an easy pace; keep the carrier (or cursor) moving steadily.

2. Take a 1' writing on each ¶; find *gwam* on each writing.

3. Take a 2' writing on all 3 ¶s combined; find *gwam*.

all letters used | E | 1.3 si | 5.2 awl | 90% hfw

gwam 1' | 2'

Establish a daily work goal; then keep it in   9 | 5
mind while you practice. Work toward it by doing   19 | 10
expertly all that is within your power to try now.   29 | 15

You do not attain success easily or quickly.   9 | 20
It costs much time and effort. There is no magic   19 | 24
road to success, now or ever. It means hard work.   29 | 30

It is a good feeling to complete whatever we   9 | 34
start to do. A major sign of our success lies in   19 | 39
what we learn through the maze of vexing problems.   29 | 44

1' | 1 | 2 | 3 | 4 | 5 | 6 | 7 | 8 | 9 | 10 |
2' | 1 | 2 | 3 | 4 | 5 |

50-space line; each line twice
SS; DS between 2-line groups
Technique Goals
- curved, upright fingers
- quick–snap keystrokes
  with fingertips

Adjacent (Side-by-Side) Reaches

```
1 we new are try was art top few aids part were lion
2 as saw oil foil ruin flop port yule silk open real
3 we try|we saw|was top|are few|were part|silk shirt
4 pop art|has oil|few ads|new port|few join|was here
5 Sally needs a few new parts to rebuild this radio.
6 Troy said we may try a few new ports on this trip.
   | 1 | 2 | 3 | 4 | 5 | 6 | 7 | 8 | 9 | 10 |
```

Technique Goals
- quiet hands and arms
- reach with the *fingers*
- wrists low

Long Direct Reaches with Same Finger

```
1 my any gun ice nut gum sun gym grin many brim hums
2 TV sum fun cent must brig dumb verb hymn herb zany
3 my gym|my pun|any sum|mud curb|many must|zany tune
4 my ace|my pace|any pun|any rice|much fun|must curb
5 A young group brought a check for the annual fund.
6 Brig must run at a fast pace to take second place.
   | 1 | 2 | 3 | 4 | 5 | 6 | 7 | 8 | 9 | 10 |
```

Technique Goals
- deeply curved fingers
- double–tap the repeated
  letter without returning
  finger to home position
  between strokes

Double-Letter Words

```
1 too all odd off see ill err zoo bee eel eggs leeks
2 inn book seen fell call keel fuzz soon hall little
3 too soon|odd fall|all eggs|bees buzz|a little jazz
4 an odd book|he will see|she teed off|she feels ill
5 Ann sees an odd inn off the road near small trees.
6 Bobbi will check off all books as she issues them.
   | 1 | 2 | 3 | 4 | 5 | 6 | 7 | 8 | 9 | 10 |
```

Alphabetic Paragraph
50–space line; DS.

1. Key the ¶ once at an easy
but steady pace.

2. Take three 1' writings on
the ¶ trying to improve your
speed. Find *gwam* on each
writing.

all letters used	E	1.2 si	5.1 awl	90% hfw

```
              .         2         .         4         .         6         .         8         .
        If you read a word ahead of the fingers when
        10        .        12        .        14        .        16        .        18        .
   you work from copy, you can recognize many letter
   20        .        22        .        24        .        26        .        28        .
   sequences that are easy and others which are hard
   30        .        32        .        34        .        36        .        38        .
   to type.  Just try next to be faster on very easy
   40        .        42        .        44        .        46        .        48        .
   groups of letters and to slow down for hard ones.
```

50-space line; DS
Capitalization

1. Read line 1 deciding what, if any, changes in capitalization need to be made.
2. Key the line with words properly capitalized.
3. Read and key each of the remaining lines in a similar way.
4. Check with your teacher the accuracy of your application of the rules.

1 have you finished the paper? it is due next week.
2 did ms. fisk request dr. and mrs. mann to help us?
3 glenda and paul briggs visited the alamo in texas.
4 does the fourth of july fall on monday or tuesday?
5 we take memorial day as a national holiday in may.
6 emery, inc., moved from spruce lane to gulf plaza.
7 our club president, louella chin, made the awards.
8 dr. mala v. cross received her m.d. from maryland.
9 j. b. evans wants to backpack in the grand canyon.
10 does your office have an apple or an ibm computer?

Spacing with Punctuation

1. Read line 1 deciding what, if any, changes in spacing need to be made.
2. Key the line leaving correct spacing after punctuation marks.
3. Check with your teacher the accuracy of your work.

1 Kim is now sixteen. She is learning how to drive.
2 She asked them to stand up, speak up, and shut up.
3 Are you going to the film? If so , may I join you?
4 Is Kevin teaching her? Or is she going to school?
5 Capitalize these words: English, French, Spanish.
6 Vic, Nan, and Kate learned to drive two years ago.
7 Order these items: two disk drives and a monitor.
8 Jo passed the driving test; Carla passed it, also.
9 I know she wants to go, but I am not sure she can.
10 I aced the written test; Al, the performance test.

Capitalization/Spacing

1. Read line 1 deciding what, if any, changes need to be made in capitalization and spacing.
2. Key the line making needed changes.
3. Check with your teacher the accuracy of your work.

1 texas and oklahoma are separated by the red river.
2 he did well in french , but he was no star in math.
3 we stopped in boise, idaho, on our way to seattle.
4 i have an appointment with ms. coe in rogers hall.
5 hugh works for ling, inc. ; janice, for davis corp.
6 as an fbla member, i am on our career day program.
7 did you see the president on tv? i was at school.
8 d.d.s. stands for doctor of dental science, i see.
9 dr. j.b. stone is on duty at university hospital.
10 john f. kennedy was a u.s. senator in those years.

50-space line
Capitalization in Sentences
1. Read each sentence, marking for correction any errors you find in capitalization.
2. Key lines 1–20, making all corrections you marked plus any you discover as you key.

1 pam molitor, our secretary, was elected president.
2 kevin will visit maine during the month of august.
3 ms. ray had an appointment with dr. chi on friday.
4 the oregon education association meets each month.
5 jay plans on leaving for colorado after labor day.
6 washington's birthday is observed during february.
7 chancellor bush returned to the office on tuesday.
8 the north concho river flows into san angelo lake.
9 is there a federal reserve bank located in denver?
10 sunshine travel agency is located on state street.
11 ms. k. c. cey, our secretary, will be the speaker.
12 president haas will announce the winner on monday.
13 their business has been moved to marquette square.
14 fbla students will tour mcdonnel computer company.
15 kay and sue will ride to the game with miss marsh.
16 she had company from boston visit on memorial day.
17 many americans will remember world war II forever.
18 the republican convention will be held in atlanta.
19 roger j. steinman is a member of delta pi epsilon.
20 london square bank has a branch located in fresno.

Capitalization in Paragraphs
1. Read each paragraph, marking for correction any errors you find in capitalization.
2. Key each paragraph, making all corrections you marked plus any you discover as you key.

dr. and mrs. c. j. nelson are planning a may trip to california to visit their daughter, sarah bergmann, who lives in oakland, california. they hope to schedule their visit over memorial day.

during their visit they will see the barbary coast, golden gate bridge, chinatown, and lombard street. their daughter has also scheduled a tour of the japanese cultural and trade center.

mrs. nelson will be attending the opening of the devny art gallery, where one of her paintings will be on exhibit. dr. nelson, a big fan of the san francisco giants, plans to see several games.

1a ▶ 35 Check
Keyboarding Technique

50-space line

Keystroking—by Rows (8')

1. Each pair of lines twice as your teacher observes and rates your technique (using the check sheet on LM pp. 13 and 14.)
2. If you finish keying before the time is called, start over.

Rows

home	1	Jud said he got a gas grill at the last fall sale.
	2	Dallas had always set high goals for Jake to make.
home/3d	3	The fresh water supply will last through the week.
	4	Joella will assist you with the play this Tuesday.
home/1st	5	Vance balanced a checkbook for Zahn back in March.
	6	Frank and Zelma have fixed scrambled eggs and lox.

Keystroking—by Fingers (8')

1. Each pair of lines twice as your teacher observes and rates your technique.
2. If you finish keying before the time is called, start over.

Fingers

1st/2d	1	ten tub bug burn crib kite here jiffy debug invite
	2	Vic might be ready to drive in the race by Friday.
3d/4th	3	so all zoo law pop saw lax low pass loss wasp soap
	4	Will Alexis allow us to play pool at Plaza Square?
all	5	Data Systems will maintain the computer equipment.
	6	The keyboarding classes will meet for eight weeks.

Spacing (8')

1. Each pair of lines twice as your teacher observes and rates your technique.
2. If you finish keying before the time is called, start over.

Spacing

words	1	am an if do or go by key may own pan pay form city
	2	to me so it us jam pen jay man firm sigh sign fury
phrases	3	if they|it is|go to the|for it|end of the|she owns
	4	pay them|six maps|risk it|he is|big rock|rich girl
sentences	5	The man owns a big dog, six ducks, and eight cows.
	6	Ruth and Kay paid the man for the map of the city.

Shifting (11')

1. Each pair of lines twice as your teacher observes and rates your technique.
2. If you finish keying before the time is called, start over.

Shift Keys and LOCK

left shift	1	Jay, Mario, Kay, Nancy, and Mike were on one team.
	2	Mary, Juan, Peter, Liz, and Larry were on another.
right shift	3	Ester, Ann, Tom, Gary, and Chi were on Team Three.
	4	Fay, Dave, Eva, Fuji, and Randy were on Team Four.
both shifts	5	W. C. McKinley and J. B. McDonnel were our guests.
	6	Dale Road, Vine Drive, and Eddy Lane are repaired.
shift lock	7	Ms. Troy belonged to NBEA, NEA, and AVA last year.
	8	Type the company name, LEWIS ADVERTISING, in caps.

1b ▶ 15 Check
Keyboarding Skill

Sentence Writings (6')
Two 1' writings on each line; find and report *gwam* on each.

alphabet 1 Val may pack a box with prized fig jams for Quent.

easy sentence 2 Hand eight land forms to the man with auburn hair.

| 1 | 2 | 3 | 4 | 5 | 6 | 7 | 8 | 9 | 10 |

Paragraph Writings (9')
1. A 1' writing on each ¶; find and report *gwam* on each.
2. Two 2' writings on ¶s 1–2 combined; find and report *gwam* on each.

all letters used | E | 1.2 si | 5.1 awl | 90% hfw | gwam 2'

If you are moving with more control now than   5

you were last week, you can be quite certain that   10

you have shown growth in keying. You can develop   15

as fast as you desire if you will work with zest.   20

For the next several days, put a little more   24

effort into your work; then check the increase in   29

speed. You will find that just a bit more effort   34

day by day can result in a much higher skill.   39

| 1 | 2 | 3 | 4 | 5 |

Optional Check on Keyboarding/Typewriting Facts

1. In the answer blank at the left of each item, write the letter of the answer that correctly completes that item.
2. Check your answers with your teacher.

_____ 1. A horizontal inch of pica (10-pitch) type has (a) 6 spaces; (b) 10 spaces; (c) 12 spaces.

_____ 2. A horizontal inch of elite (12-pitch) type has (a) 6 spaces; (b) 10 spaces; (c) 12 spaces.

_____ 3. Paper that is 8½ inches wide has (a) 66; (b) 85; (c) 102 elite (12-pitch) horizontal spaces per line.

_____ 4. Paper that is 8½ inches wide has (a) 66; (b) 85; (c) 102 pica (10-pitch) horizontal spaces per line.

_____ 5. When keying in single-spaced mode, (a) 0; (b) 1; (c) 2 vertical line spaces are left between lines.

_____ 6. When keying in double-spaced mode, (a) 0; (b) 1; (c) 2 vertical line spaces are left between lines.

_____ 7. Elite (12-pitch) type is (a) larger than pica type; (b) smaller than pica type; (c) the same size as pica type.

_____ 8. When elite (12-pitch) type is used, the paper guide should be set so that the horizontal center of a sheet of paper 8½ inches wide is (a) 42; (b) 51; (c) 66.

_____ 9. When pica (10-pitch) type is used, the paper guide should be set so that the horizontal center of a sheet of paper 8½ inches wide is (a) 40; (b) 42; (c) 51.

_____ 10. A standard sheet of typing paper, which is 11 inches long, has (a) 33; (b) 50; (c) 66 vertical line spaces.

50-space line; SS
To improve control of new keys and motions:
1. Key each line of a 4–line drill twice: first, slowly; then faster.
2. Key each line of a 4–line drill once more at a brisk but comfort–able pace.

Lesson 26: 1 and 7

1 1 la la lla lla ala ala; Reach to the 1 key quickly.

7 2 7j 7j 77j 77j j7j j7j; I can key 7 and 77 quickly.

1/7 3 Do you want 17 or 117? He learned when he was 17.

1/7 4 I have a brother 17, one sister 11, and another 7.

Lesson 27: 4 and 8

4 1 4f 4f 44f 44f f4f f4f; Reach to 4, then down to f.

8 2 8k 8k 88k 88k k8k k8k; Reach to 8, then down to k.

4/8 3 Of 84 members, 48 were at the meeting on August 4.

all figures learned 4 Answers to Items 17 and 18 are on pages 47 and 48.

Lesson 28: 5 and 9

5 1 5f 5f 55f 55f f5f f5f; I can key 5 and 55 quickly.

Use the letter "l" 9 2 9l 9l 99l 99l l9l l9l; Reach to 9, then down to l.

5/9 3 Key these figures: 5, 9, 55, 99, 59, 95, and 559.

all figures learned 4 We had 857 workers in 1984; by 1987, we had 1,154.

Lesson 29: 3 and 0 (zero)

3 1 3d 3d 33d 33d d3d d3d; Reach to 3, then down to d.

0 2 0; 0; 00; 00; ;0; ;0; Can he key 0 and 00 quickly?

3/0 3 Key the figures 3, 0, and 303. See page 30 or 33.

all figures learned 4 I bought 1,750 acres in 1958; in 1987, I sold 340.

Lesson 30: 2 and 6

2 1 2s 2s 22s 22s s2s s2s; I can key 2 and 22 quickly.

6 2 6j 6j 66j 66j j6j j6j; Quickly key 6, 66, and 666.

2/6 3 Ms. Hix was 62 on May 26; she will retire June 26.

all figures used 4 I know the figures: 0, 1, 9, 2, 8, 3, 7, 4, 6, 5.

To master reaches to the figure keys:
1. Key each line twice: first, slowly; then faster.
2. Take a 1' writing on each line to improve speed; find *gwam* on each line.

Figure Review (all figures used in each line)

1 Key 10 and 29 and 38 and 47 and 56 at a fast pace.

2 We tried next 105 and 294 and 383 and 472 and 561.

3 Use a comma: 1,203 and 2,394 and 3,485 and 6,275.

4 The club met from 5 to 6:30 p.m., August 24, 1987.

5 In 1982 they had only 105 computers; by 1987, 364.

| 1 | 2 | 3 | 4 | 5 | 6 | 7 | 8 | 9 | 10 |

60-space line

Skill Transfer Sentences

1. A 1' writing on each line of each pair; find *gwam*.

2. Compare rates; then take two more 1' writings on the slower line of the pair.

Goal: 75% of alphabet line rate on figure line.

% of transfer = rate on figure copy ÷ rate on alphabetic copy

Skill Transfer Sentences

alphabet	1	Jan was to give Rex Buckholtz a quiet party before he moved.
figures	2	My home number is 836-4197 and my office number is 832-9057.
alphabet	3	Marjie gave the exquisitely designed black gown for a prize.
figures	4	Only 1,893 of the 4,650 reserved seats were sold by June 27.
alphabet	5	Dawn Jeltz quickly gave up because of the extreme penalties.
figures	6	His 9:30 and 10:30 classes were in Hibbard Hall 427 and 586.
alphabet	7	Vicky Zawski appeared in time for judging the quilt exhibit.
figures	8	I graduated in 1985 with 207 credits and a 3.64 grade point.

| 1 | 2 | 3 | 4 | 5 | 6 | 7 | 8 | 9 | 10 | 11 | 12 |

Skill Transfer Paragraphs

1. A 1' writing on each ¶ of a 2-¶ set; find *gwam* on each writing.

2. Compare rates; then take two more 1' writings on the slower ¶ of the set.

Goal: 75% of alphabet ¶ rate on figure ¶.

% of transfer = rate on figure ¶ ÷ rate on alphabet ¶

Skill Transfer Paragraphs

all letters/figures used | E | 1.2 si | 5.1 awl | 90% hfw

Set 1   Being able to work well with others is quite a crucial trait for one to have in the business world of today. The degree of success with any job you may have depends on just how well you can excel with the field of human relations.

Those who recognize the need and value of getting along with others are those who move to the top very quickly. It is quite simple to show your eagerness to work with others. You can do so with a smile that lasts all day long.

Set 2   In 1960 nearly 40 percent of the Americans who were 25 years of age or over had finished high school. By 1970 this changed to 80 percent. It is quite amazing that it took just 10 years to see such a change exist.

There has been a change in the number of college grad-uates, too; but this change has not been as huge. It took 30 years for the 5 percent of college graduates in 1940 to change to 12 percent in 1970.

60-space line

Response Patterns

1. Each line twice: first, slowly; then faster. Follow this plan:

Lines 1-3 (think–say–key the words by letter response)

Lines 4-6 (think–say–key the words by word response)

Lines 7-9 (use top speed for easy words, lower speed for more difficult ones)

2. A 1' writing on line 10; find *gwam*; then on line 11 and on line 12 in the same way.

Response Patterns

letter	1	my joy gas ink data hook edge lion base milk card kill after
	2	my car | bad debts | cedar tree | phony art | nylon dress |water polo
	3	After Edwards restated my facts, a minimum rate was created.
word	4	if end jam kept goal hand fuel chair digit laugh aisle blame
	5	six firms | their social | right angle | the auditor | the oak chair
	6	Their busy neighbor may go to a social held by the sorority.
combination	7	own are land crew name link when join they milk shelf street
	8	big tree | ivory vase | eight acres | their union | a severe problem
	9	The cedar ornament on the bare shelf was their only antique.
letter	10	In my opinion, Dave acted better after we gave him a rebate.
word	11	The man with the bicycle also owns a shanty by the big lake.
combination	12	Bob decreased the minimum fuel reserve and created problems.

| 1 | 2 | 3 | 4 | 5 | 6 | 7 | 8 | 9 | 10 | 11 | 12 |

Figure Drills

1. Each line twice: first, slowly; then faster.

2. A 1' writing on each of lines 3, 6, and 9; find *gwam* on each.

Figure Drills

1 to 30 be 41 me 73 at 68 go 57 we 23 it 93 as 20 do 46 she 18
2 19 states | 21 seconds | 80 inches | 13 minutes | 45 years | 67 points
3 The 15-point quiz on January 27 covers pages 38, 49, and 60.

4 the 309 and 418 say 275 day 639 are 804 you 152 too 796 pies
5 409 yards | 610 miles | 147 points | 120 months | 365 days | 198 women
6 Check Numbers 267, 298, 304, and 315 were still outstanding.

7 gone 7183 said 2964 like 5013 bikes 9403 your 7894 were 6775
8 4,873 prizes | 1,500 copies | 2,460 miles | 1,389 cars | 6,872 seats
9 Only 1,473 of the 6,280 members were at the 1985 convention.

| 1 | 2 | 3 | 4 | 5 | 6 | 7 | 8 | 9 | 10 | 11 | 12 |

Skill Transfer

1. A 1' writing on ¶ 1; find *gwam*.

2. A 1' writing on ¶ 2; find *gwam*.

3. Compare *gwam* on the two ¶s; two 1' writings on the slower ¶ to increase speed.

Skill Transfer

all letters/figures used | E | 1.2 si | 5.1 awl | 90% hfw

The group using the 34 elite machines was told to set
their machines at 21 and 86 for a line length of 60 spaces.
Just 5 extra spaces are added at the right side for the bell.
The ones using the 19 very old pica machines were told to
set margins quickly at 12 and 77 for the same size line length
since their machines have 10 spaces to an inch rather than 12.

60-space line

Spacing with Punctuation Marks

1. Check lines 1–10 for errors in spacing; circle each error.
2. Key lines 1–10, correcting each spacing error you found.

Spacing with Punctuation Marks

1 The meeting is scheduled for Friday,April 18, at 10: 30 a. m.
2 Dr. Jones arrived in Dallas on March 9; he left on March 15.
3 Steven's height was 6ft. ; however, he weighed only 140lbs.
4 Jo was tested on the following: letters,memos, and tables.
5 Dr.Devan received his P h. D. at Michigan State in chemistry.
6 Their editor, T.J. Martell, informed them of the due dates.
7 He used these words correctly: accept,effect,and capitol.
8 She was born on July 14,1985, at 5:30 a. m. in Oxbow, Maine.
9 Rafael abbreviated Tues.,Wed.,and Thurs. in this schedule.
10 Marsha left her home at 11 : 30 a.m. for her 1:30 p.m. flight.

Capitalization

1. Check lines 1–10 for errors in capitalization; circle each error.
2. Key lines 1–10, correcting each capitalization error you found.

Capitalization

1 The Fbla members elected j. b. Ryan as their next President.
2 Did Mr. and Mrs. Gunderson move to new Mexico or to Arizona?
3 The october tour included visits to paris, rome, and naples.
4 The next OEa meeting is scheduled for saturday, september 9.
5 Bart and Kay plan on spending christmas skiing at park city.
6 first financial bank will be located at 1025 Charles avenue.
7 Exquisite geysers can be found in Yellowstone national park.
8 the doctors elected dr. Jay Massoth as their Representative.
9 Dr. Chan parked in front of the Civic Center on star avenue.
10 Pedro went to Mexico City to spend christmas with his Uncle.

Number Expression

1. Check lines 1–10 for errors in number expression; circle each error.
2. Key lines 1–10; correcting each number expression error you found.

Number Expression

1 1 more book was bought to bring the total purchased to twenty-five.
2 The six phones he ordered on May 5 were delivered on July 1.
3 4 of the 5 starters on his team were six ft. two in. tall.
4 Lessons eight and nine give 12 rules for use in expressing numbers.
5 10 of the 16 individuals listed were contacted on August first.
6 The September 12 meeting is scheduled to begin at ten thirty a.m.
7 Order six roses, 12 carnations, and six tulips from the florist.
8 The last flight from Denver arrived at 6:38 p.m. at Gate ten.
9 Nine sophomores, six juniors, and 12 seniors were in the play.
10 The instructor assigned Chapters six and seven to his 12 students.

ENRICHMENT ACTIVITY 13:
Keyboard Learning—Symbols

Use after completing designated lessons.

60-space line

1. Key each line of a 4–line drill twice: first, slowly; then faster.

2. Key each line of a 4–line drill once more at a brisk but comfortable pace.

Lesson 33: / (diagonal) and $ (dollars)

/ 1 /; /; ;/; ;/; 1/4 plus 1/4 equals 2/4 or 1/2; 4/8 equals 1/2

$ 2 $f f$f f $4 $f $ I owe Jo $4, Dee $7, Jay $7, and Jill $3.

/ and $ 3 Your invoices dated 4/16/87 and 5/16/87 amounted to $186.88.
4 The diamond cost $600; the garnet, $350; and the ruby, $200.

Lesson 34: % (percent) and - (hyphen)

% 1 % % 5% 8% 6% He scored 85%, 75%, and 99% on the three tests.

- 2 -- -; -; -;- ;- first-class, twenty-two, May 1-4, pages 9-13

% and - 3 The three banks quoted interest rates of 8.7%, 9%, and 8.5%.
4 His social security number was 520-56-2899, not 520-57-2899.

Lesson 35: # (number, pounds) and & (ampersand, and)

1 # d#3 d# #3 3# 3 Sheila drew #26, #28, and #15 from the box.

& 2 &j& J&J & 7&8 & 3&4 j&j Tay is employed by Cox & Jones, Inc.

and & 3 Diaz & Chan finished #1; Fox & Soto, #2; and Cey & Epps, #3.
4 The class will learn to key #3 & #7 today; #5 & #9 tomorrow.

Lesson 36: (and) [left and right parentheses]

(1 (L9 3(3 (5L(Use the right third finger to key (1, (2, & (3.

) 2);0 2)2);) Use the right little finger to key 1), 2), & 3).

(and) 3 Dee had three accounts (#165, #289, and #304) with our bank.
4 Nelson (Ken) and Smyth (Jeff) were given the Murphy account.

Lesson 37: ' (apostrophe) and " (quotation mark)

' 1 ' '; ';' ': ': 's 'll 've 'm it's I'll I've I'm I'll go too.

" 2 " "; ";" ": ": "You can buy one," the clerk said, "not two."

' and " 3 "I'm having difficulty," Pam said, "keying the z's and x's."
4 "Practice writing both your 7's and 8's," Mrs. Presley said.

Lesson 38: __ (underline) and * (asterisk)

— 1 _; _;_ _: _;_ ; _:_ Use the underline key for word emphasis.

* 2 *k *8 *k* *8* *3* What is the * on the telephone used for?

— and * 3 The * can be used to denote a footnote at the end of a page.
4 The * after his name denotes he set the record in 162 games.

Symbol Review

1 The firm (Goldberg & Bush) paid their secretary $12.50/hour.

2 Cindy's theme, "Today's Leaders," received 90% of the votes.

3 This model (#8*73H) is on sale during the week of June 9-14.

To improve technique as you key the three lines:
Keep fingers curved, upright.
Keep hands quiet.
Reach with the fingers.

Enrichment Activity 13: Keyboard Learning—Symbols

ENRICHMENT ACTIVITY 14:
Language Skills

60-space line

Spacing with Punctuation, Numbers, and Symbols

1. Check lines 1–10 for errors in spacing; circle each error.

2. Key lines 1–10, correcting each spacing error you found.

Spacing with Punctuation, Numbers, and Symbols

1 The twins (Kammi&Kerrie)weighed 6 1 / 2 lbs. and 6 1 / 4 lbs.

2 The adjustable interest rate was 10 1/2% as of September12.

3 The real estate agency (Hanson & Meyer Realty, Inc.) closed.

4 The next game was scheduled for 7:35 p. m. on Friday,May 15.

5 Dr. Kim -- the art instructor -- was the recipient of the award.

6 The invoice(# 8291) dated 10 /8/ 85 for $ 399 was still unpaid.

7 Twenty - three members voted for my amendment; three,against.

8 Dr. Carlson will be on vacation during the week of June 1 -8.

9 Jerome J. Satz, M. D.,is a physician at Schofeld Clinic Ltd.

10 Please phone Ms. Perkins in San Francisco at (415) 782-4316.

Number Expression

1. Check lines 1–10 for errors in number expression; circle each error.

2. Key lines 1–10, correcting each number expression error you found.

Number Expression

1 Minneapolis is located in UPS Zone two; Sacramento, in Zone seven.

2 Eight of the thirteen members were on time for the 7 a.m. meeting.

3 Rhonda and Daniel bought the home located at 1 Gibbs Lane.

4 Martin's office is located downtown at twelve Washington Square.

5 The exam was scheduled to take fifty minutes; I finished in 39.

6 The two men in charge (Fox & Grayson) will be here at nine a.m.

7 UPS charged Tim $3.30 to deliver the package weighing six lbs.

8 Week one will be spent on graphics and Week two on spreadsheets.

9 The 12 new computers arrived in time for the May 8 workshop.

10 Cleo ordered six copies for Don, two for Tom, and 12 for Carmen.

Capitalization

1. Check lines 1–10 for errors in capitalization; circle each error.

2. Key lines 1–10, correcting each capitalization error you found.

Capitalization

1 I am sure that Gary Nelson works at 125 Philadelphia square.

2 The premium on Policy no. 8725 should be paid before friday.

3 Anita Wyler was elected Treasurer of the Club for next year.

4 The bus stops at the corner of Sixth avenue and Vine street.

5 Prime minister thatcher flew to Washington, d.c., on June 9.

6 The American heart association will assist with the program.

7 The christmas party was held at 9 Lincoln avenue on tuesday.

8 The conference will be held march 12-14 in atlanta, georgia.

9 Mary and i saw Mt. rushmore during our stay in south dakota.

10 Nashville, the capital of tennessee, is by old hickory lake.

60-space line

Problem 1 (2 half sheets)
Centered Announcements

Begin on line 10; center each line horizontally; DS the lines. See textbook p. 68 for procedure, if necessary.

Lesson 39: Centered Announcements

Eighth Annual
Frosty Eve Holiday Dance
Friday, December 13, 19--
8:30 p.m. - 1:00 a.m.
High School Gymnasium
$3.50 per person

Downtown Business Association
Guest Speaker: Erin Gray
Topic: Secretaries--The Endangered Species
March 15, 19--
8:00 p.m.
Civic Center Inn

Problem 2 (half sheet)
Personal Note

Format the note as illustrated on textbook p. 70. Use your name in the closing lines.

Lesson 41: Personal Note

February 8, 19--

Dear Betty

Last month at the convention in Kansas City, you mentioned that you were interested in attending a workshop next summer on computer applications. I just received a flier from Pace Business College announcing their summer programs.

They are offering one-week workshops on graphic applications, electronic spreadsheets, and word processing software packages. If you are interested, I will request more information.

Sincerely

Problem 3 (half sheet)
Simplified (Informal) Memo

Format the memo as illustrated on textbook p. 72. Use your name in the closing lines.

Lesson 42: Simplified (Informal) Memo

December 1, 19--

Business Education Teachers

SPEAKER FOR DECEMBER FBLA MEETING

Please announce in your classes that Mr. Todd Lefebvre will be the guest speaker for the December FBLA meeting. He is the Director of Human Resources for Griffin, Seymour & Company. His topic, "Preparing for the Job Interview," should be of interest to all graduating seniors.

The meeting will be held on Monday, December 8, at 4:30 p.m. in the auditorium. We hope that you and your students will join us for Mr. Lefebvre's presentation.

(your name), FBLA President

60-space line

1. Key ¶ 1 for 1'. If you complete it within the minute, move to ¶ 2 for the next timing, and so on.

If you are unable to complete a ¶ within the minute, rekey it until you do. If you complete a ¶ before time is called, start over.

2. Take a 2' writing on ¶s 1–5. Find *gwam*; circle errors.

3. Take a 3' writing on ¶s 1–5. Find *gwam*; circle errors.

4. Take a 2' writing on ¶s 6–8. Find *gwam*; circle errors.

5. Take a 3' writing on ¶s 6–8. Find *gwam*; circle errors.

6. If your teacher directs, take a series of 1' *guided* writings on selected ¶s.

Quarter-Minute Goals

gwam	¼'	½'	¾'	Time
20	5	10	15	20
24	6	12	18	24
28	7	14	21	28
32	8	16	24	32
36	9	18	27	36
40	10	20	30	40
44	11	22	33	44
48	12	24	36	48
52	13	26	39	52
56	14	28	42	56

all letters used | LA | 1.4 si | 5.4 awl | 85% hfw

gwam 2' | 3'

¶ 1 Learning to key without wasting time and effort demands 6 | 4
a great deal of practice of the proper kind. 10 | 7

¶ 2 I shall soon experience quite effective uses for my new 16 | 11
skill. That is one of the major reasons for learning to key. 22 | 15

¶ 3 During the next few months, I will master the keying of 28 | 18
social and business papers. Perhaps, then, they will dub me 34 | 23
a real expert. 35 | 24

¶ 4 Reports, letters, and tables are among the tasks I must 41 | 27
master now. According to one recent study, these are simple 47 | 31
jobs that I must do very well. 50 | 34

¶ 5 My speed may indeed drop as I change from straight copy 56 | 37
to other jobs. Therefore, I must remember to employ my best 62 | 41
work habits for every job, whatever its size. 67 | 44

¶ 6 Skill developed on copy used up to this time will stand 6 | 4
me in really good stead. Of particular aid will be my skill 12 | 8
in using the return and tabulator, and the backspacer, also. 18 | 12

¶ 7 Learning to key is rough work; however, the skill built 24 | 16
makes my time well spent. If following a better method will 30 | 20
speed progress, I will pursue it. I need sufficient ability 36 | 24
to do a top job. 38 | 25

¶ 8 When I key letters, reports, or tables, the time needed 43 | 29
for planning my work and getting my machine ready for keying 49 | 33
will lower my speed. As a result, I should learn to do each 55 | 37
of these steps efficiently. 58 | 39

gwam 2' | 1 | 2 | 3 | 4 | 5 | 6
3' | 1 | 2 | 3 | 4

Chesapeake State Bank

723 S. Charles Street • Baltimore, MD   21230-3820 • (301) 741-3600

47c, Problem 2, page 84

InfoTronics, Inc.

115 W. Seventh Street • Fort Worth, TX 76102-2160 • (817) 561-3640

48c, Problem 3, page 86

Royalty Foods, Inc.

7200 Ocean Boulevard, E
Long Beach, CA 90803-3842

Royalty Foods, Inc.

7200 Ocean Boulevard, E • Long Beach, CA   90803-3842 • (213) 871-5050

60-space line
date: line 15

Problem 1
Personal-Business Letter

Format the letter shown at the right on a plain full sheet in block style with open punctuation. Refer to textbook p. 75 for formatting guides, if needed. Check finished copy for errors and circle each error you find.

words

7425 Mobile Street | Houston, TX 77011-4622 | May 7, 19-- | 11
Ms. Cheryl Bryant, Manager | The Light House | 2396 Maryknoll   23
Drive | Houston, TX 77015-3190 | Dear Ms. Bryant   32

Last week I purchased a dining room light fixture from The   43
Light House. When I unpacked the light at home, I found a   55
polished brass fixture had been sent instead of an antique   71
brass fixture. I phoned Mr. Braxton, the salesperson from   80
whom I purchased the light, to ask what I should do. He   91
was very reassuring and told me the correct fixture would be   102
shipped immediately. It arrived today in perfect shape.   114

I want you to know, Ms. Bryant, that it is because of   125
sales personnel like Mr. Braxton, that I continue to   135
return to The Light House for all my lighting needs. Your   147
sales staff has always been excellent.   155

Sincerely | Miss Jillian Kramer   160

Problem 2
Business Letter

On a letterhead (LM p. 59) or on a plain full sheet, format the letter shown at the right in block style with open punctuation. Refer to textbook p. 75 for formatting guides, if necessary. Check finished copy for errors and circle each error you find. Address a large envelope (see textbook p. 83 for addressing procedures, if necessary).

May 9, 19-- | Ms. Roberta Long | Farrell Equipment Company | 11
6392 Saint Andrews Way | Seattle, WA 98112-5872 | Dear Ms. Long   23

Here is the proposal you requested for the installation of a   35
word and information processing center. We are confident that   48
our product, our support specialists, and our services will   60
fully meet your needs.   65

We are proposing a totally integrated information system which   77
is easy to learn, has excellent technical capabilities, and   90
allows for possible growth. Our support specialists will be   101
glad to demonstrate the features of this system to you at   113
your convenience.   117

The possibility of working with Farrell Equipment Company on   129
this project is exciting for us. Thank you again for inviting   142
us to submit a proposal. Hopefully, this will be the begin-   154
ning of a long business partnership.   161

Sincerely | Leonard Leslie | Sales Manager | xx | Enclosure   171

ENRICHMENT ACTIVITY 18:
Review—Formatting Notes, Memos, and Lists

60-space line

Problem 1 (half sheet)
Personal Note

Format the note in block style; use your name in the closing lines. See textbook p. 70, if necessary, for assistance. Check your finished copy for errors; circle each error you find.

	words
February 20, 19--	4
Dear Betty	6

I contacted Pace Business College to learn more about their summer course offerings. It appears that a couple of the workshops will fit into your summer plans. — 18 / 30 / 38

During the week of July 7-11, they are offering a course on word processing software packages. The next week, July 14-18, the course on electronic spreadsheets is being offered. The graphic applications course will not be offered until the first week of August. — 51 / 64 / 77 / 89 / 91

I have requested that they send you additional information about their programs. — 104 / 108

Sincerely — 109

Problem 2 (half sheet)
Simplified (Informal) Memo

Format the memo in block style. See textbook p. 72, if necessary, for assistance. Check your finished copy for errors; circle each error you find.

	words
October 3, 19--	3
All Faculty	6
GRADE REPORTS	8

The first grading period is quickly approaching. Next week, you will be receiving a grade reporting form for each of your classes. This form should be completed and turned in to the school secretary by Tuesday, October 15. — 21 / 35 / 48 / 54

I will meet with all new faculty on Tuesday, October 8, at 4:15 p.m. in the faculty conference room to explain the grading form. At that time, I will also be happy to respond to any questions that returning faculty may have about the procedure. — 66 / 80 / 93 / 103

James Q. Rosenberg, Principal — 109

Problem 3 (half sheet)
Numbered List

Format the list in simple report style. See textbook p. 69, if necessary, for assistance. Check your finished copy for errors; circle each error you find.

OPSCAN GRADING FORM INSTRUCTIONS — 7

1. Use a black pen to write in letter grades. — 16

2. Use a #2 pencil to blacken in the grade circle that corresponds with the letter grade you have assigned. — 28 / 38

3. To record the number of absences, use a #2 pencil to blacken in the circle. — 50 / 54

4. Be sure to fill all circles completely. — 63

5. Do not use any correction device other than the eraser for correcting pencil errors. — 77 / 82

6. Do not write on the back side of the form. — 92

7. Be sure to sign the form with a black pen after completing. — 105

ENRICHMENT ACTIVITY 19:
Self-Check Questions—Personal Notes, Memos, Lists, and Letters
Use after completing Lesson 48.

1. In the answer blank at the left of each item, write the letter of the answer that correctly completes that item.
2. Check your answers with the key inside the back cover of this book.

_____ 1. When all lines of a personal note or a letter are begun at the left margin, the document is said to be formatted in (a) block style; (b) modified block style; (c) simplified style.

_____ 2. When a personal note or a simplified memo is prepared on a half sheet with the long edge at the top, place the date on line (a) 6; (b) 7; (c) 8.

_____ 3. Between the date and salutation of a personal note, space down (a) 2 times; (b) 3 times; (c) 4 times.

_____ 4. Between the date and receiver's name of a simplified memo, space down (a) 2 times; (b) 3 times; (c) 4 times.

_____ 5. Paragraphs of personal notes and simplified memos are usually (a) single-spaced; (b) double-spaced; (c) triple-spaced.

_____ 6. When paragraphs are single-spaced, they are separated by (a) a single space; (b) a double space; (c) a triple space.

_____ 7. When the writer's name is keyed in a personal note, it is separated from the complimentary close by a (a) double space; (b) triple space; (c) quadruple space.

_____ 8. Between the last line of the body of a simplified memo and the writer's name, leave a (a) double space; (b) triple space; (c) quadruple space.

_____ 9. When a numbered list is placed on a half sheet with the long edge at the top, center the heading on line (a) 6; (b) 7; (c) 8.

_____ 10. Between the heading of a numbered list and the first paragraph or numbered item, space down (a) 2 times; (b) 3 times; (c) 4 times.

_____ 11. Individual items in a numbered list are usually (a) single-spaced; (b) double-spaced; (c) triple-spaced.

_____ 12. When numbered items in a list are individually single-spaced, they are usually separated from one another by a (a) single space; (b) double space; (c) triple space.

_____ 13. Figures used to identify items in a numbered list are followed by (a) 1 space; (b) 2 spaces; (c) 3 spaces.

_____ 14. When no punctuation follows any of the opening or closing lines in a letter, the punctuation style is called (a) closed; (b) mixed; (c) open.

_____ 15. When all lines of a personal or business letter begin at the left margin, the letter is said to be formatted in (a) block style; (b) modified block style; (c) simplified style.

_____ 16. Between the date and address of a letter, space down (a) 2 times; (b) 3 times; (c) 4 times.

_____ 17. Between the complimentary close and the keyed name of the writer, space down (a) 2 times; (b) 3 times; (c) 4 times.

_____ 18. Between the letter address and the salutation, space down (a) 1 time; (b) 2 times; (c) 3 times.

_____ 19. Between the salutation and the body of a letter, space down (a) 1 time; (b) 2 times; (c) 3 times.

_____ 20. Between the paragraphs of a letter, (a) single-space; (b) double-space; (c) triple space.

_____ 21. Between the body and complimentary close of a letter, (a) single-space; (b) double-space; (c) triple-space.

_____ 22. Closing lines beneath the writer/department name line(s) are (a) single-spaced; (b) double-spaced; (c) triple-spaced.

_____ 23. When addressing a small envelope, begin the address (a) 5 spaces; (b) 10 spaces; (c) 15 spaces to the left of horizontal center of envelope.

_____ 24. When addressing a large envelope, begin the address (a) 5 spaces; (b) 10 spaces; (c) 15 spaces to the left of horizontal center of envelope.

_____ 25. When addressing a large envelope, begin the address on (a) line 12; (b) line 14; (c) line 16.

ENRICHMENT ACTIVITY 20:
Language Skills

60-space line

Capitalization, Number Expression, and Spacing

1. Read each sentence, marking for correction any errors you find in capitalization, number expression, and spacing.

2. Key lines 1–25, making all corrections you marked plus any you discover as you key.

1 ms. roselawn said,"you have twelve minutes to finish the exam."

2 "I can paint the entire house, "he said," In only 6 days."

3 the test on chapters twelve and 13 covers pages 128 through 178.

4 major rex johnson took a taxi from 6th street to broadway.

5 about 1/5 of the members voted for the grahn proposal.

6 kay took a bus to one kingston drive for the one p. m. meeting.

7 ellen's baby was 32 inches long and weighed almost nine pounds.

8 four of the 6 winners were from the jefferson art gallery.

9 mary j. fox will present the award to dr.chang at 9:30 a. m.

10 " You can learn the software package," i said,"in twelve hours."

11 twelve of the 33 participants were Seniors; 21 were juniors.

12 charles made five free throws and six baskets to score 17 points.

13 the dog show featured 12 Collies, 8 poodles, and seven terriers.

14 delegates from Iowa, idaho,and maine voted no on the issue.

15 the exhibit sponsored by key photo club was very successful.

16 the awards banquet for OEA will be held on tuesday, april nine.

17 kay and jill were skiing at lake tahoe over christmas break.

18 they stayed at yellowstone national park for four full days.

19 the end for our team is six ft. three in. tall and weighs 230 lbs.

20 coach davis advised us to Be mentally prepared for the game.

21 the first place winner,paul hanold,is from topeka, kansas.

22 the arts fair sponsored by fbla will be held at carson park.

23 the special guests included governor jones and mayor nelson.

24 mr. and mrs. j.b. hutterli were the 1st guests to arrive.

25 the next pi omega pi meeting will be held on wednesday, march 17.

Word Division

As you key each line, insert a hyphen at each point at which each word can be acceptably divided.

1 fabric, self-respect, icebox, ideas, four, hourly, button

2 validate, reliable, flood, chemical, flexible, current

3 adult, enjoyable, critical, definable, elect, blizzard

4 misspell, even, wouldn't, clerical, neighbor, birthstone

5 self-sufficient, nightgown, haven't, deductible, blotter

6 well-being, wasn't, venison, eighty, escapable, flounder

7 amend, expendable, summer, discount, open-ended, doesn't

8 keepsake, chance, across, don't, sandwich, supply, surely

ENRICHMENT ACTIVITY 21:
Compose-at-the-Machine Drills

60-space line; DS

Drill 1
Short Response Questions

1. List the numbers 1–10 at the left margin.
2. Read Question 1. Opposite the number 1 on your paper, key a 1– to 5–word response to the question.
3. Read and complete the other items in the same way.

1. What is your name?
2. What is your street address, route number, or box number?
3. In what city (or county) and state do you live?
4. What is your ZIP Code number?
5. What is your telephone number?
6. What is your area code?
7. In what town, city, or county were you born?
8. In what month and year were you born?
9. In what school grade are you now?
10 In what year do you expect to be graduated?

Drill 2
Sentence Completion

1. List the numbers 1–10 at the left margin.
2. Read Statement 1. Opposite the number 1 on your paper, key the sentence, filling in the material indicated in parentheses.
3. Read and complete the other items in the same way.

1. I attend (insert name of school).
2. I am learning to key in a course called (insert name).
3. The name of my textbook is (insert title).
4. My textbook has (insert number) authors.
5. The company which published my book is (insert name).
6. The copyright year of the book is (insert year).
7. I am learning to key on a (insert typewriter or computer).
8. The brand name of my machine is (insert name).
9. The type size of the machine is (insert pica or elite).
10. My machine is (insert a manual, an elecric, or an electronic).

Drill 3
Sentence Completion

1. List the numbers 1–10 at the left margin.
2. Read Statement 1. Opposite the number 1 on your paper, key the sentence, filling in your response.
3. Read and complete the other items in the same way.

1. My favorite city is _____.
2. My favorite state is _____.
3. My favorite television star is _____.
4. My favorite sports figure is _____.
5. My favorite food is _____.
6. My favorite subject is _____.
7. My favorite song is _____.
8. My favorite movie is _____.
9. My favorite sport is _____.
10. My favorite month is _____.

ENRICHMENT ACTIVITY 21:
Compose-at-the-Machine Drills, continued

60-space line; DS

Drill 4
Sentence Composition

Select five of the ten questions in Drill 4. Compose a sentence or two in response to each of the five questions; include the number of the question with your answer.

1. If you had a million dollars, what would you do with it?
2. Where would you like to go on your next vacation?
3. If you could live anywhere, where would you choose?
4. What is your favorite season? Explain why.
5. What do you enjoy doing in your spare time?
6. What is your favorite pet?
7. Describe your school.
8. What is your favorite holiday? Why?
9. Why are you taking this keyboarding course?
10. What is the most difficult part of learning to keyboard?

Drill 5
Sentence Composition

Select five of the ten questions in Drill 5. Compose in a sentence or two a response to each of the five questions; include the number of the question with your response.

1. What do you like best about school?
2. What do you like least about school?
3. What do you plan to do after you are graduated from school?
4. If you had one wish, what would you wish for?
5. What qualities do you like most about your best friend?
6. What are your hobbies?
7. What is your most important accomplishment in life?
8. Name as many states as you can that start with the letter M.
9. Name as many states as you can that have double letters in their names.
10. Name the first President of the United States.

Drill 6
Sentence Composition

Select three of the five items in Drill 6. Compose several sen–tences in response to each of the three items; include the number of the item in your response.

1. Tell about a current event that is taking place in the world today and give your opinion about it.
2. If you had a choice of being a famous sports figure, a movie star, or a politician, which would you choose? Why?
3. What is your favorite television program? Explain why it is your favorite program.
4. Are grades or extracurricular activities more important to you? Why?
5. If school were cancelled for a week, what would you do during that week?

Unique Gardens, Inc.
4199-57th Street
Des Moines, IA 50310-4729

49c, Problem 2, page 88

Unique Gardens, Inc.

4199-57th Street • Des Moines, IA   50310-4729 • (515) 472-3600

Unique Gardens, Inc.
4199-57th Street
Des Moines, IA 50310-4729

49c, Problem 3, page 88

Unique Gardens, Inc.

4199-57th Street • Des Moines, IA   50310-4729 • (515) 472-3600

2a ▶ 6 Conditioning Practice

1. Each line twice SS.
2. A 1' writing on line 3; find *gwam*.

alphabet 1 Jack and Mary Vasquez will purchase the eight boxes of eggs.

fig/sym 2 The taxes (1985) were $932 on the $74,000 home on Oak Drive.

speed 3 Their rich neighbor owns the land on the island in the lake.

| 1 | 2 | 3 | 4 | 5 | 6 | 7 | 8 | 9 | 10 | 11 | 12 |

2b ▶ 7 Check Keyboarding Skill: Straight Copy

1. A 1' writing on ¶ 1, then on ¶ 2; find *gwam*, circle errors.
2. A 3' writing on ¶s 1 and 2 combined; find *gwam*, circle errors.

all letters used | A | 1.5 si | 5.7 awl | 80% hfw

gwam 2' | 3'

It is extremely important to use extra care in addressing 6 | 4

envelopes. By doing so, you will make it easier for the mail 12 | 8

to be processed quickly. Because of the automation being used 18 | 12

with mail today, certain requirements have to be met to assure 25 | 16

rapid processing. 27 | 18

The correct format and placement of the return address 32 | 21

and destination address on the envelope are very important. 38 | 25

Just as important as the correct placement and format of the 44 | 29

addresses is the ZIP Code. If it is not included, your mail 50 | 34

will not be delivered nearly as fast. 54 | 36

gwam 2' | 1 | 2 | 3 | 4 | 5 | 6 |
3' | 1 | 2 | 3 | 4 |

2c ▶ Check Keyboarding Skill: Statistical Copy

1. A 1' writing on ¶ 1, then on ¶ 2; find *gwam*, circle errors.
2. A 3' writing on ¶s 1 and 2 combined; find *gwam*, circle errors.

all letters/figures used | A | 1.5 si | 5.7 awl | 80% hfw

gwam 2' | 3'

The jovial real estate agent described the quaint house 6 | 4

at 2608 Nimitz Avenue, which was just placed on the market last 12 | 8

week, as being an immaculate home in perfect condition. The 18 | 12

upper level of the home has 1,194 square feet. 23 | 15

The home, which was built in 1979, is exquisitely decorated 29 | 19

on the inside and very beautifully landscaped on the outside. 35 | 23

The wooded lot on which the home is located measures 150 feet 41 | 27

by 135 feet. 42 | 28

gwam 2' | 1 | 2 | 3 | 4 | 5 | 6 |
3' | 1 | 2 | 3 | 4 |

2d ▶ 29 Check
Formatting Skill
Problem 1 (LM p. 71)
Business Letter

line: 60
format: block style
date: line 15
Listen for bell to return; correct errors.

words

January 5, 19-- Mrs. Marcia L. Hamby 2638 Silver Oaks Way   12
Spring Valley, CA 92077-4830 Dear Mrs. Hamby   21

I am glad you will be able to meet me in San Diego to discuss the   34
position of sales representative in the Southern California area.   48

While in San Diego, I shall stay at the Town & Country Hotel.   60
Why don't you meet me there for lunch at 11:30 on January 20. If   74
either the suggested time or place is not convenient for you, we   87
can make other arrangements for the interview.   96

As soon as I arrive in San Diego on January 18, I shall telephone   109
you to confirm the interview appointment.   118

Sincerely yours Rollin C. Vandalia National Sales Manager xx   130

Problem 2 (plain half sheet)
Simplified Memo

line: 60
date: line 15
format: block style
Listen for bell to return; correct errors.

November 16, 19-- Production Unit Supervisors TEXT-EDITING   12
DEMONSTRATION   15

Ms. Janine Kemp will be here on November 28 to demonstrate   26
the new Zeus Text-Editor that we are considering for use in the   39
editorial department.   44

Please mark your calendar to keep 1:30 to 4:00 open on Monday   56
afternoon, November 28. If for any reason you are unable to   68
attend this important demonstration, let me know immediately.   81

Ramon Rivera, Managing Editor xx   87

Problem 3 (plain full sheet)
Personal-Business Letter

line: 60
date: line 15
format: block style
Listen for bell to return; correct errors.

2640 Las Olas Boulevard, E. Fort Lauderdale, FL 33301-7265 De-   12
cember 4, 19-- Mr. Byron K. Simms, Manager Centronic Office   24
Machines, Inc. 15 Columbus Circle New York, NY 10023-8952   36
Dear Mr. Simms   39

Thank you for sending me the material on keyboarding champ-   51
ions that I requested. The posters my committee prepared based   63
on the material have created much interest among the keyboard-   76
ing students.   79

It is hard to believe that anyone can key 149 words a minute for   92
an hour! Such speed makes our rates of 25 to 40 words a minute   104
for 3 minutes seem poor, but many of us are now determined to   117
do better.   119

We really appreciate your sharing this information with us.   131
Maybe someday one of us will be a champion and be featured on a   144
"Keyboarding Champions" poster.   151

Sincerely yours Rilla Raintree   157

Progress Checkup 2, Problem 1, LM page 70

Buckeye Insurance Company
300 Madison Avenue • Toledo, OH 43604-1842

Buckeye Insurance Company

300 Madison Avenue • Toledo, OH   43604-1842 • (419) 781-4646

68b-70b, Job 4, page 121 (Letter 1)

Kilmer Youth Camp

P.O. Box 575 • Tapoco, NC 28780-8514

Kilmer Youth Camp

P.O. Box 575 • Tapoco, NC 28780-8514 • (704) 482-3711

Kilmer Youth Camp
P.O. Box 575 • Tapoco, NC 28780-8514

68b-70b, Job 4, page 121 (Letter 2)

Kilmer Youth Camp

P.O. Box 575 • Tapoco, NC 28780-8514 • (704) 482-3711

68b-70b, Job 4, page 121 (Letter 3)

Kilmer Youth Camp
P.O. Box 575 • Tapoco, NC 28780-8514

Kilmer Youth Camp

P.O. Box 575 • Tapoco, NC 28780-8514 • (704) 482-3711

Kilmer Youth Camp
P.O. Box 575 • Tapoco, NC 28780-8514

68b-70b, Job 4, page 121 (Letter 4)

Kilmer Youth Camp

P.O. Box 575 • Tapoco, NC 28780-8514 • (704) 482-3711

73c., Problem 2, page 126

Buckeye Insurance Company
300 Madison Avenue • Toledo, OH 43604-1842

83

Buckeye Insurance Company

300 Madison Avenue • Toledo, OH   43604-1842 • (419) 781-4646

Buckeye Insurance Company
300 Madison Avenue • Toledo, OH 43604-1842

73c, Problem 3, page 126

Buckeye Insurance Company

300 Madison Avenue • Toledo, OH   43604-1842 • (419) 781-4646

3a ▶ 7 Conditioning Practice

1. Each line twice SS.
2. A 1' writing on line 3; find *gwam*.

alphabet 1 Panicked by her very low quiz score, Mae just about forgot to see Rex.

fig/sym 2 Invoice # 26784 was for $152.90 (139 quarts of oil at $1.10 per quart).

speed 3 A city auditor and six girls may go by bus to work with the lake firm.

| 1 | 2 | 3 | 4 | 5 | 6 | 7 | 8 | 9 | 10 | 11 | 12 | 13 | 14 |

3b ▶ 7 Check Keyboarding Skill: Straight Copy

1. A 1' writing on ¶ 1, then on ¶ 2; find *gwam*, circle errors on each writing.
2. A 3' writing on ¶s 1 and 2 combined; find *gwam*, circle errors.

all letters used | A | 1.5 si | 5.7 awl | 80% hfw

gwam 2' | 3'

The amazing automated office of the future that was just talked · 6 | 4 | 49
about in the past is now today's office. The vast advances that have · 13 | 9 | 53
been taking place in the word and data processing arena in the last few · 21 | 14 | 58
years have quickly changed the office. In spite of the previous improve- · 28 | 19 | 63
ments, it is expected that rapid advances in these areas will continue. · 35 | 23 | 68

Since the automated office of the future is here, experts are pro- · 42 | 28 | 72
jecting to the future. Voice data entry is expected to be one of the · 49 | 33 | 77
next major changes in office technology. Even though systems currently · 56 | 37 | 82
exist with voice data entry, major improvements will have to be made · 63 | 42 | 86
before they are common in the office. · 67 | 44 | 89

gwam 2' | 1 | 2 | 3 | 4 | 5 | 6 | 7
3' | 1 | 2 | 3 | 4 | 5

3c ▶ 7 Check Keyboarding Skill: Statistical Copy

1. A 1' writing on ¶ 1, then on ¶ 2; find *gwam*, circle errors on each writing.
2. A 3' writing on ¶s 1 and 2 combined; find *gwam*, circle errors.

all letters used | A | 1.5 si | 5.7 awl | 80% hfw

gwam 2' | 3'

Numbers are very important to learn. Just as much care and atten- · 7 | 4 | 39
tion should be given to learning numbers as is devoted to learning the · 14 | 9 | 44
rest of the keyboard. Street addresses (3740 Iris Avenue) and dates · 21 | 14 | 49
(July 24, 1986) are two of the ways numbers are frequently used. · 27 | 18 | 53

Other usages of numbers include Zip Codes (98101-2932) and tele- · 34 | 22 | 58
phone numbers (504-318-7645). Expert typists should be as certain in · 41 | 27 | 62
keying a number as they are in keying a letter. They should try for at · 48 | 32 | 67
least 70 percent of their alphabetic copy rate. · 53 | 35 | 70

gwam 2' | 1 | 2 | 3 | 4 | 5 | 6 | 7
3' | 1 | 2 | 3 | 4 | 5

3d ▶ 25
Check Capitalization, Number Expression, and Word Division

60-space line; DS
Problem 1
Capitalization

1. Check lines 1–10 for capitalization errors, marking each error for correction.
2. Key lines 1–10, correcting the errors you have marked.

1 The Singing Statesmen will perform at roosevelt high school.
2 The speaker was an instructor from dallas, mrs. Jane Robins.
3 The three finalists were from arizona, nevada, and kentucky.
4 Jay and Dave were going to meet at McIntyre Library at noon.
5 There are branches of the firm in spain, Germany, and japan.
6 The information should be in either chapter I or chapter II.
7 The first stoplight after Harrison Lane is at second avenue.
8 The President of the group was not at the meeting on monday.
9 Richard carney works for meyer & james, the Accounting firm.
10 The summer months of june, july, and august were very humid.

Problem 2
Number Expression

1. Check lines 1–10 for errors in number expression, marking each error for correction.
2. Key lines 1–10, correcting the errors you have marked.

1 Is their new address four Robertson Road or 1218 Corridon Park?
2 Twenty-five students applied for the internship at the bank.
3 The tallest girl in the senior class, Gail, was five ft. 11 in.
4 Three of the 9 days will be spent in Seattle, Washington.
5 The memo dated March six, 1986, included 2 of the estimates.
6 The duplicated materials should be ready in about 5 days.
7 Only 1/3 of the members attended the previous meeting.
8 The interest rate was changed from ten 3/4 to eleven 1/2 percent.
9 There are 2 flights, 1 at 9:30 a.m. and 1 at two:48 p.m.
10 The new house they bought will be ready in 1 or 2 weeks.

Problem 3
Word Division

Set left margin for a 60–space line. Set margin stops 14, 31, and 44 spaces to the right of the margin. As you key each line DS, insert a hyphen at the point at which each word can be acceptably divided.

1 various	experience	you're	shipment
2 request	purchase	weather	apparently
3 electric	technical	system	established
4 able	management	payment	organize
5 average	carefully	computer	corporation
6 business	processing	legal	association
7 family	literature	crossing	opportunity
8 volume	president	without	telephone
9 remember	investment	year	possibility
10 success	agreement	letter	profession

PROGRESS CHECKUP 4:
Formatting Letters

Use after completing Lesson 75.

4a ▶ 10
Conditioning Practice

1. Each line twice SS.
2. A 1' writing on line 4; find *gwam*.

alphabet 1 Jessica and Elizabeth very quickly explained the forgeries to Matthew.

figures 2 "The test will cover pages 87-106 as well as pages 243-295," she said.

fig/sym 3 The cost of the chair (Model #6415) and desk (Model #370) was $528.79.

speed 4 The dismal shanty on the island was the handiwork of the eighty girls.

| 1 | 2 | 3 | 4 | 5 | 6 | 7 | 8 | 9 | 10 | 11 | 12 | 13 | 14 |

4b ▶ 40 Check
Formatting Skills: Letters

1 letterhead (LM p. 91)
2 plain full sheets
Problem 1 (plain full sheet)
Personal-Business Letter
line: 60
format: block style, open
date: line 15
Use your own return address; correct any errors you make.

words

April 6, 19- - ... 3

Dr. Marsha Sedgwick ... 7
Garrison Business College ... 12
2879 Mapleton Avenue ... 16
Boulder, CO 80301-4824 ... 21

Dear Dr. Sedgwick ... 25

I am interested in taking the Certified Professional Secre- ... 36
tarial Examination in the next year. Victoria Ramos suggested ... 49
that I contact you for information on the review course that ... 61
your department offers for the CPS Exam. She took the course ... 74
several years ago and indicated that it was very helpful ... 85
to her in preparing for the exam. ... 92

I am hoping to take the review course during the summer--is it ... 105
offered? If not, is there another course offered this summer ... 117
that would be helpful in preparing for the examination? ... 128

The thought of going back to school again is very appealing to ... 141
me. Please send me the information as soon as possible. ... 153

Sincerely ... 155

Miss Rita Hawthorne ... 159

xx ... 159

Problem 2 and 3 are on page 90.

4b, continued
Problem 2 (LM p. 91)
Business Letter
line: 60
format: block style, open
date: line 15
Correct all marked errors
and any errors you make
as you key the letter.
Prepare an envelope.

words

December 20, 19-- 4

Ms. Marilyn Nuesse 7
The Gibbon Information Center 13
1486 Basswood Lane 17
St. Louis, MO 63132-3481 22

Dear Ms. Nuesse 26

I apreciate you taking the time tohave your staff demon- 37
strate the integrated information processing system to 48
me on friday. It certainly appears to have all the *vital* 59
capabilities that our support staff feels are ~~necessary~~. 69

Mr. Nelson roraff, our word processing supervisor, and 80
Ms. Alyssa Franks, our data processing supervisor, would 92
like to observe the system and further discuss some of 103
our unique requirements with your staff members. Would 114
it be possible for them to meet with you shortly after 125
the holidays? Please telephone Mr. Roraffs or Ms. Frank 136
at 837-6211 to arrange a time for their visit. 146

Sincerely 148

Conrad Rinaldi 151
Vice President 154

xx 154

Problem 3 (plain full sheet)
Format and key the letter in
Problem 1 again, but address it to:
Dr. Reese Marichal
Newberry Business College
3817 Zenobia Way
Denver, CO 80219-6380
In the body of the letter, change
the name of **Victoria Ramos**
to **Sondra Locks.** Supply an
appropriate salutation.

InfoTronics, Inc.

115 W. Seventh Street • Fort Worth, TX 76102-2160

Progress Checkup 4, Problem 2, LM page 90

InfoTronics, Inc.

115 W. Seventh Street • Fort Worth, TX 76102-2160 • (817) 561-3640

5a ▶ 10
Conditioning
Practice

1. Each line twice SS.
2. A 1' writing on line 4; find *gwam*.

alphabet 1 Joe very quickly called Chuck just before swimming a dozen extra laps.

figures 2 Dee moved from 3872 Cedar Road to 5406 Aster Lane in the fall of 1985.

fig/sym 3 His account (#8256) was debited for $130.49 for December 17 purchases.

speed 4 The problem with the giant oak chair in the chapel is the shape of it.

| 1 | 2 | 3 | 4 | 5 | 6 | 7 | 8 | 9 | 10 | 11 | 12 | 13 | 14 |

5b ▶ 40
Check Formatting
Skills: Reports

Format and key the copy shown at the right and on page 94 as an unbound 2–page report. Format the reference list on a separate sheet.

As you key, correct all marked errors and any errors you make as you key.

words

Today's Office Worker   4

There are many opportunities in the business world   15

for qualified office workers. Depending on the source,   26

it is estimated that there are *currently* between 250,000 and 500,000   40

openings today. As industry moves from manufacturing to   50

more service-oriented businesses, the demand for office   61

support staff is likely to increase.   69

Much of the shortage has been attributed to the fact   79

that women are now entering professions which were *previously* domi-   93

nated by men. The salary has also been another *a* negative   101

factor for individuals looking at an office career; How-   112

ever, salaries are starting to increase *ing*. This is par-   121

ticularly true in the area of word processing *support personnel*. Cecil   135

(1984, p. 316) states that firms are willing to pay *skilled* good   147

word processing personnel more because they are more   157

productive.   160

Increased office automation provides the office   170

worker with a more challenging job and the opportunity   181

for advancement to higher-level positions. In larger   191

companies, the traditional duties *of the secretary* have been separated.   206

The duties of support personnel are either classified as   217

administrative or word processing, opening two avenues   228

for advancement.   232

(continued on page 94)

5b, continued

Administrative *Duties* 241

    The starting position in the administrative area may 251
require taking dictation and transcribing from notes or 262
dictation equipment, handling trav~~ile~~ ar~n~angements, screen- 274
ing calls, answering routine~^correspondence^~ ~~mail~~, making appointments, 287
and maintaining fil~e~ing systems. As an individual advances 299
to a higher level, a ^greater^ knowledge of company polic~ies~y and 311
procedure~s~ and above-average secretarial and administrative 323
skills are needed. A top-level administrative position 334
will require a person to relieve an executive of ^routine^ adminis- 347
trative detail (McFarland, 1985, ~~pp~~ 14-15). 356

Word Processing *Duties* 365

    The starting position in the area of word processing 375
~~calls for~~ *requires* the person to use word processing equipment to 387
input, edit, customize, and deliver medium-to-complex ^typed^ 399
documents with established quality and ^time^ standards. The 411
more advanced jobs in word processing require~s~ the indi- 422
vidual to produce and revise complicated documents. This 433
may include lengthy technical and statistical reports 444
which require retrieval and integration of ~~text~~ *data* with ~~data~~ *text* 456
(McFarland, 1985, p 15). 460

REFERENCES 2

Cecil, Paul B. <u>Office Automation Concepts and Applica-</u> 21
    tions. Menlo Park, CA: The Benjamin/Cummings 31
    Publishing Company, 1984. 37

McFarland, Emmett. <u>Secretarial Procedures: Office</u> 53
    <u>Administration and Automated Systems.</u> Reston, VA: 70
    Reston Publishing Company, Inc., 1985. 78

PROGRESS CHECKUP 6:
Formatting Tables/Centering

6a ▶ 10
Conditioning Practice
1. Each line twice SS.
2. A 1' writing on line 4; find *gwam*.

alphabet	1	Major Knight relaxed after passing both quizzes with very high scores.
figures	2	The baseball team drew 1,806,211 at home and only 953,740 on the road.
fig/sym	3	I ordered 18 diskettes ($3.90 ea.) and 26 cartridge disks ($4.75 ea.).
speed	4	The enchantment of the downtown chapel kept the visitor on the island.

| 1 | 2 | 3 | 4 | 5 | 6 | 7 | 8 | 9 | 10 | 11 | 12 | 13 | 14 |

6b ▶ 40 Check Formatting Skills: Tables/Centering
Problem 1 (half sheet)
Announcement

Center the announcement verti–cally on a half sheet DS; center each line horizontally.

words

Ninth Annual — 3

Business Ethics Seminar — 7

Guest Speakers: Reed Crosby and Kayleen La Fontaine — 18

Tuesday, October 28, 19--, 7 p.m. — 25

Carlton House — 28

Sponsored by the Accounting Association — 35

Problem 2 (half sheet)
2-Column Table with Main and Secondary Headings

SS columnar entries; 20 spaces between columns; correct any errors you make.

QUIZ ON FREQUENTLY MISSPELLED WORDS — 7

January 30, 19-- — 11

		words
privilege	equipped	14
withhold	forfeit	18
acknowledgment	analyze	22
grievance	brochure	26
convenience	achievement	31
financial	apologize	35
illegal	judgment	38
questionnaire	notarize	43
ridiculous	tragedy	47
urgent	voluntary	50
accommodate	separate	54
believable	diversity	59
amendment	itinerary	62

6b, continued
Problem 3 (full sheet)
3-Column Table with Main, Secondary, and Column Headings

DS columnar entries; decide spacing between columns; correct any errors you make as you key the table.

words

BARSTOW CLINIC — 3

Physician Roster — 6

Name	*Specialization*	*Phone*	16
Dr. Ruth Bitzer	*General Surgery*	*834-7650*	24
Dr. Steven Freitag	*Internal Medicine*	*834-9365*	34
Dr. Maria Gutierrez	*Family Practice*	*834-1736*	43
Dr. Ruben Khatib	*Pediatrics*	*834-6524*	50
Dr. Brett Nelson	*Psychiatry*	*834-3091*	57
Dr. Thomas Vulstek	*Allergy*	*834-2891*	65
Dr. Marleen Wahl	*Family Practice*	*834-2551*	73
Dr. Vernon Young	*Pediatrics*	*834-3819*	80

Problem 4 (full sheet)
3-Column Table with Headings and Source Note

DS columnar entries; decide spacing between columns; correct any errors you make as you key the table.

EVENING SCHOOL COURSE <u>enrollments</u> — 7

Business education Department — 13

BSED 350	Business Communications	23	20
BSED 306	Business Report Writing	14	27
BSED 315	Word Processing Applications	25	35
BSED 316	Records Management	28	42
BSED 317	Administrative Management	26	49
BSED 423	Administrative Support Concepts	21	58
BSED 508	Seminar in Administrative *Management*	7	68
BSED 732	Business Research	12	74

77

source: Registrars Report, September 25, 19--. — 86